M000250557

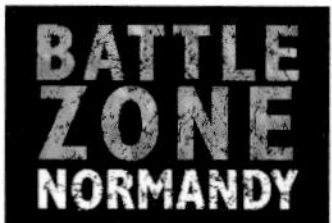

BATTLE FOR CHERBOURG

The 'Battle Zone Normandy' Series

Orne Bridgehead Lloyd Clark
Sword Beach Ken Ford
Juno Beach Ken Ford
Gold Beach Simon Trew
Omaha Beach Stephen Badsey & Tim Bean
Utah Beach Stephen Badsey
Villers-Bocage George Forty
Battle for Cherbourg R.P.W. Havers
Operation Epsom Lloyd Clark
Battle for St-Lô Nigel de Lee
Battle for Caen Simon Trew
Operation Cobra Christopher Pugsley
Road to Falaise Stephen Hart
Falaise Pocket Paul Latawski

All of these titles can be ordered via the
Sutton Publishing website
www.suttonpublishing.co.uk

The 'Battle Zone Normandy'
Editorial and Design Team
Series Editor Simon Trew
Senior Commissioning Editor Jonathan Falconer
Assistant Editor Nick Reynolds
Cover and Page Design Martin Latham
Editing and Layout Donald Sommerville
Mapping Map Creation Ltd
Photograph Scanning and Mapping Bow Watkinson
Index Michael Forder

BATTLE ZONE NORMANDY

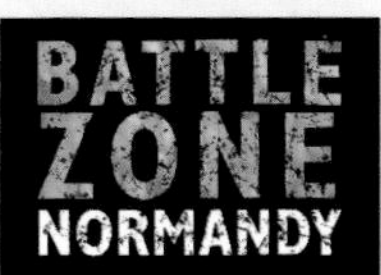

BATTLE FOR CHERBOURG

R.P.W. HAVERS

Series Editor: Simon Trew

Foreword:
Colonel J.D. Morelock

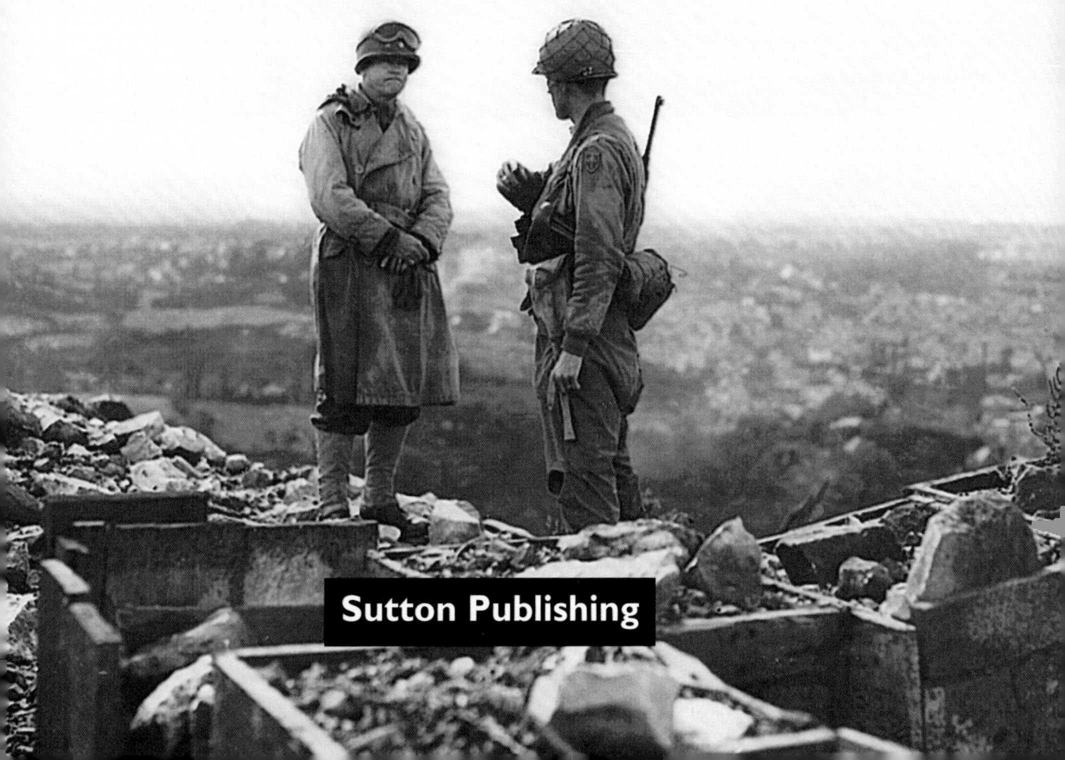

Sutton Publishing

First Published in 2004 by
Sutton Publishing Limited · Phoenix Mill
Thrupp · Stroud · Gloucestershire · GL5 2BU

British Library Cataloguing in Publication Data
A catalogue record for this book is available from The British Library.

ISBN 0-7509-3006-3

Typeset in 10.5/14 pt Sabon

Printed and bound in England by
J.H. Haynes & Co. Ltd, Sparkford

Front cover: A German soldier surrenders amid the ruins of Cherbourg. *(United States National Archives [USNA])*

Page 1: The memorial at Barneville-Carteret to the cutting of the Cotentin Peninsula by 9th US Infantry Division. *(Author)*

Page 3: To the victor the spoils: Maj Gen Collins and an officer from 314th Infantry Regiment atop the ruins of Cherbourg's Fort du Roule. The whole city is spread out in the background, illustrating the dominating position the fort held. *(USNA)*

Page 7: M4 Sherman tank cautiously negotiating the rubble-strewn streets of Cherbourg. *(USNA)*

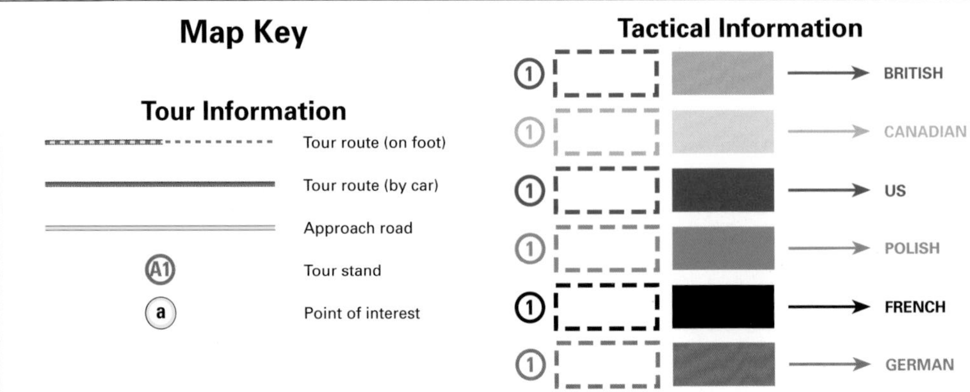

CONTENTS

THE NORMANDY BATTLEFIELD

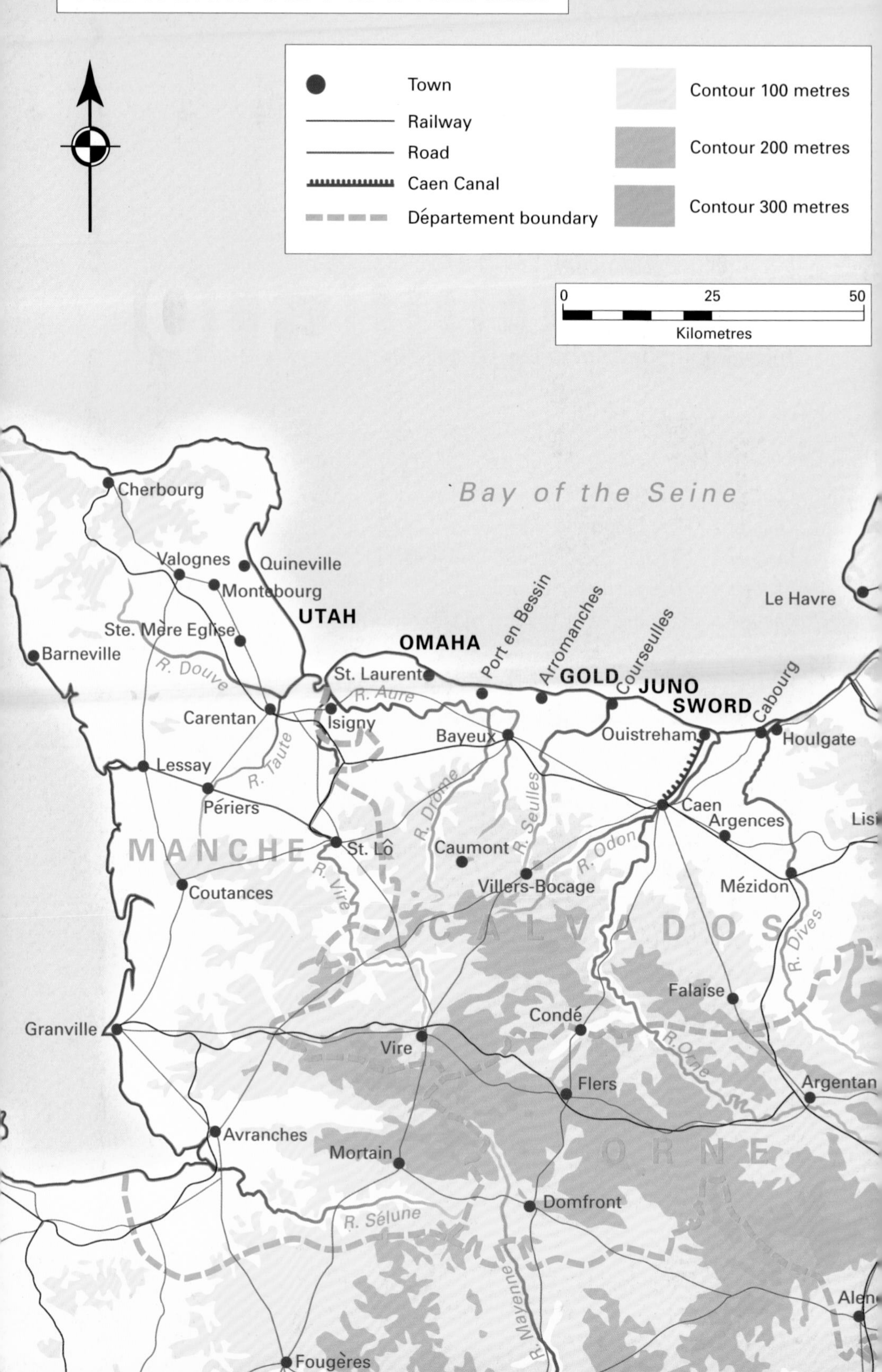

PART ONE

INTRODUCTION

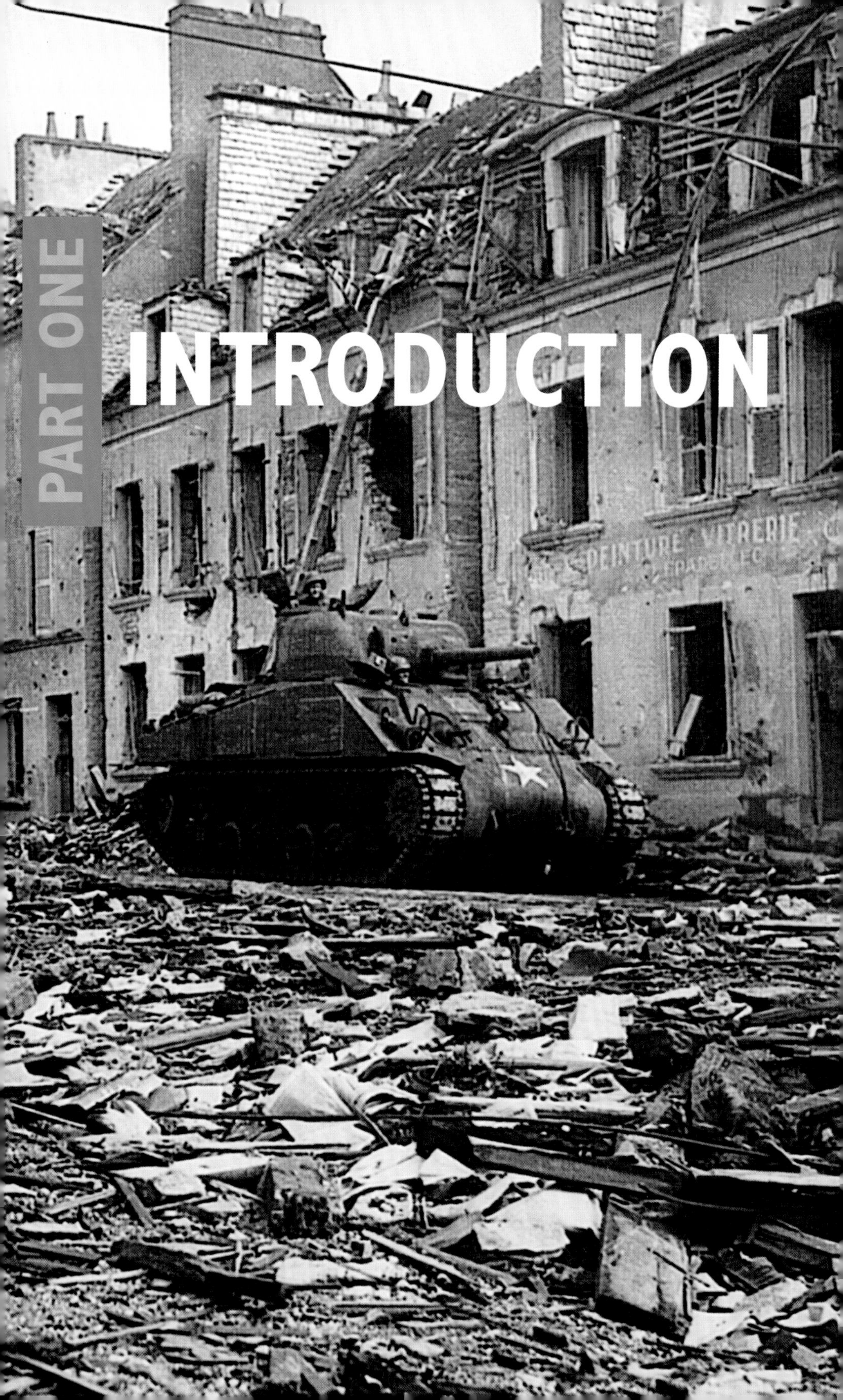

BATTLE ZONE NORMANDY

The Battle of Normandy was one of the greatest military clashes of all time. From late 1943, when the Allies appointed their senior commanders and began the air operations that were such a vital preliminary to the invasion, until the end of August 1944, it pitted against one another several of the most powerful nations on earth, as well as some of their most brilliant minds. When it was won, it changed the world forever. The price was high, but for anybody who values the principles of freedom and democracy, it is difficult to conclude that it was one not worth paying.

I first visited Lower Normandy in 1994, a year after I joined the War Studies Department at the Royal Military Academy Sandhurst (RMAS). With the 50th anniversary of D-Day looming, it was decided that the British Army would be represented at several major ceremonies by one of the RMAS's officer cadet companies. It was also suggested that the cadets should visit some of the battlefields, not least to bring home to them the significance of why they were there. Thus, at the start of June 1994, I found myself as one of a small team of military and civilian directing staff flying with the cadets in a draughty and noisy Hercules transport to visit the beaches and fields of Calvados, in my case for the first time.

I was hooked. Having met some of the veterans and seen the ground over which they fought – and where many of their friends died – I was determined to go back. Fortunately, the Army encourages battlefield touring as part of its soldiers' education, and on numerous occasions since 1994 I have been privileged to return to Normandy, often to visit new sites. In the process I have learned a vast amount, both from my colleagues (several of whom are contributors to this series) and from my enthusiastic and sometimes tri-service audiences, whose professional insights and penetrating questions have frequently made me re-examine my own assumptions and prejudices. Perhaps inevitably, especially when standing in one of Normandy's beautifully-maintained Commonwealth War Graves Commission cemeteries, I have also found myself deeply moved by the critical events that took place there in the summer of 1944.

'Battle Zone Normandy' was conceived by Jonathan Falconer, Commissioning Editor at Sutton Publishing, in 2001. Why not, he suggested, bring together recent academic research – some of which challenges the general perception of what happened on and after 6 June 1944 – with a perspective based on familiarity with the ground itself? We agreed that the opportunity existed for a series that would set out to combine detailed and accurate narratives, based mostly on primary sources, with illustrated guides to the ground itself, which could be used either in the field (sometimes quite literally), or by the armchair explorer. The book in your hands is the product of that agreement.

The 'Battle Zone Normandy' series consists of 14 volumes, covering most of the major and many of the minor engagements that went together to create the Battle of Normandy. The first six books deal with the airborne and amphibious landings on 6 June 1944, and with the struggle to create the firm lodgement that was the prerequisite for eventual Allied victory. Five further volumes cover some of the critical battles that followed, as the Allies' plans unravelled and they were forced to improvise a battle very different from that originally intended. Finally, the last three titles in the series examine the fruits of the bitter attritional struggle of June and July 1944, as the Allies irrupted through the German lines or drove them back in fierce fighting. The series ends, logically enough, with the devastation of the German armed forces in the 'Falaise Pocket' in late August.

Whether you use these books while visiting Normandy, or to experience the battlefields vicariously, we hope you will find them as interesting to read as we did to research and write. Far from the inevitable victory that is sometimes represented, D-Day and the ensuing battles were full of hazards and unpredictability. Contrary to the view often expressed, had the invasion failed, it is far from certain that a second attempt could have been mounted. Remember this, and the significance of the contents of this book, not least for your life today, will be the more obvious.

Dr Simon Trew
Royal Military Academy Sandhurst
December 2003

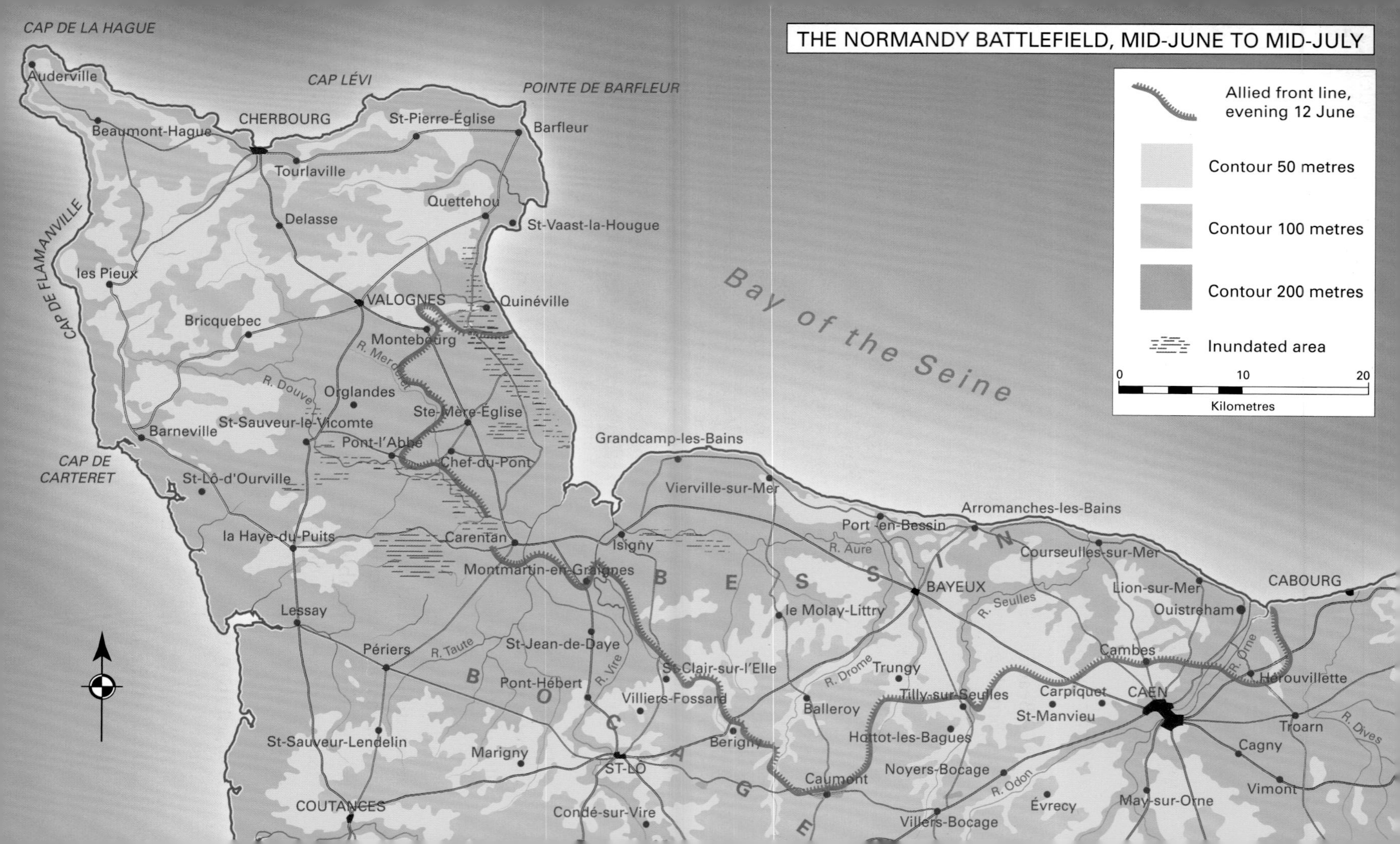

THE NORMANDY BATTLEFIELD, MID-JUNE TO MID-JULY

FOREWORD

The intense combat that characterized the opening hours of the Normandy invasion – the bloody battle at Omaha Beach, the dramatic paratroop landings behind Nazi lines, British glider-borne infantry seizing the Orne bridges, the Rangers' scaling the sheer cliffs of Pointe du Hoc – tend to make us forget that Operation 'Overlord' was, in essence, a logistics operation. As Professor Martin Blumenson once patiently explained to a younger colleague, the sole purpose of the invasion was to establish a massive and unassailable logistics base on the European continent that would then arm, fuel, supply, and man the subsequent Allied drive to defeat Nazi Germany. When studied within the context of Overlord's main purpose, the campaign to seize Cherbourg was clearly *not* an unnecessary diversion of combat power, but instead represented the very linchpin of the Allied effort. Indeed, the subsequent failures of the Allies rapidly to capture and open other major ports, such as Brest in Brittany and later Antwerp, have served to emphasize the absolutely crucial role that the port of Cherbourg played.

Professor Robin Havers' examination of the crucial battle for Cherbourg manages to get at the very heart of the struggle for this important objective of the Overlord operation, and he skilfully demonstrates how this key victory was accomplished. Significantly, this volume describes the struggle from both perspectives – the US attackers' and the German defenders' – to provide a complete picture of how the fighting progressed. In the process, Havers is able to highlight some of the important challenges that faced the commanders of both sides, but most particularly the Americans. The capture of Cherbourg was led by one of the most dynamic and successful corps commanders who emerged from the ranks of US combat leaders in World War II, Major General J. Lawton 'Lightning Joe' Collins. Collins, whose post-World War II career culminated in his rise to become Chief of Staff of the US Army, turned out to be the spark plug whose aggressive leadership of VII US Corps in the European campaign made his corps the engine that drove the entire First US Army to its battlefield successes in France and Germany. First US Army's commanders, Lieutenant General Omar Bradley and, later, Lt Gen Courtney Hodges, relied heavily on Collins' dynamic leadership. Havers' story of Collins' command of the Cherbourg campaign shows clearly how the VII US Corps commander's leadership developed to become crucial to their success.

Havers' narrative of the struggle for Cherbourg also shows the weaknesses exhibited by the US Army in its early battles on the European continent, particularly his description of the problems of the troubled 90th US Infantry Division. Tentative and over-cautious, the 90th struggled time and again to overcome stiff German resistance, and was frequently unable to keep up the pace of advance set by Collins. The 90th Division's difficulties during the Cherbourg campaign epitomized one of the major criticisms of the US Army's operations in Europe; that is, the American insistence on substituting overwhelming firepower for battlefield maneuver. The 90th's failures were typical manifestations of this shortcoming. In fact, the 90th was never consistently able to achieve its objectives until after several of its division commanders, key staff officers, and regimental commanders had been relieved for cause; it finally found success under Major General Raymond McLain. Under his leadership, the 90th was at last molded into a successful unit, and it performed well in the final months of the war. McLain became the highest-ranking National Guard (the American term for Territorial Army) officer in the European Theater of Operations, ending the war as a lieutenant general and corps commander.

This volume is an outstanding reference and guide to one of the most important campaigns of the entire Overlord plan, and it is invaluable to those who wish to supplement their study of this important part of World War II history by visiting the actual scenes of these actions. Read this volume and the other military histories recommended by Professor Havers, walk the actual terrain over which the campaign for Cherbourg was fought, and then reflect on the actions of the soldiers and commanders on both sides. This represents the best method for truly understanding this vital campaign.

J.D. Morelock, PhD
Colonel, US Army, ret.

PART TWO

HISTORY

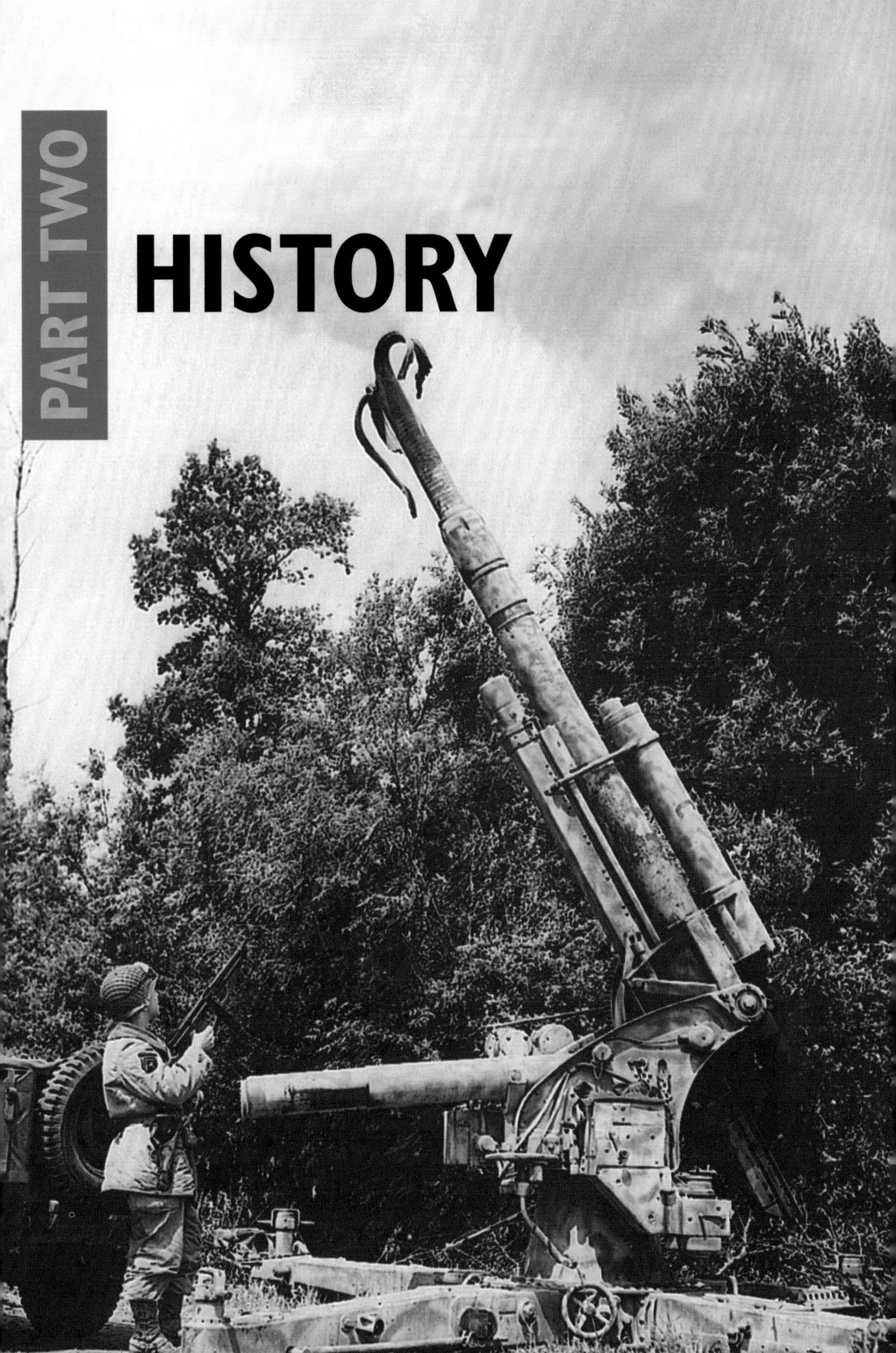

CHAPTER 1

THE STRATEGIC CONTEXT

On 6 June 1944 the Western Allies, Great Britain, the USA, Canada and the French government in exile under General de Gaulle, launched Operation 'Overlord', an amphibious operation on a hitherto unimagined scale. The purpose of Overlord, beginning with its assault phase Operation 'Neptune', was to put ashore sufficient military forces to liberate occupied Europe and to defeat the armies of Nazi Germany, thereby destroying Adolf Hitler's Third Reich. The Allies disregarded the most direct invasion route, across the Channel at its narrowest point opposite the heavily fortified Pas de Calais (a landing area that also offered the most direct route into Germany's industrial heartland of the Ruhr). They opted instead for the Lower Normandy region of France with its open beaches and comparatively weak German defences.

By the evening of 6 June, courtesy of a combination of good fortune and plentiful reserves of courage and fortitude, Allied troops had landed across five beaches on the Normandy coast from the mouth of the River Orne in the east to the eastern shores of the Cotentin peninsula in the west. These beaches were code-named (in order, west to east) 'Utah' and 'Omaha', where the Americans landed, and 'Gold', 'Juno' and 'Sword' where the British and Canadian forces came ashore. Operation Neptune was a triumph on very many levels with the myriad problems of an opposed landing against prepared enemy positions having been overcome. Just landing such a force was merely the beginning of the exercise, however. The task of provisioning such a force, a force that was growing every day, was an enormous one. The Allied armies in Normandy required tremendous amounts of food and ammunition and their vehicles required fuel and spare parts. The vast Allied superiority in men and matériel would mean nothing if its strength could not be translated into fighting power and this power brought to bear on the enemy.

Above: Allied Supreme Commander General Dwight D. Eisenhower and a pensive-looking Maj Gen J. Lawton Collins, who led the capture of the well-defended port city of Cherbourg, consider the next stage of the battle, 4 July. *(USNA)*

Page 13: An American soldier examines a German 88-mm anti-aircraft gun, used in Normandy to such devastating effect in both its designated role and as an anti-tank weapon. This particular example, photographed on 20 June outside Montebourg, has been 'spiked' by its retreating German crew. *(USNA)*

It had been realised early on in the planning for the invasion that, within days of the landing, the massive logistical requirements of the Allied armies would outstrip the limited capability provided by unloading supplies across open beaches. In the short term these problems were to be addressed by the employment of enormous artificial harbours, code-named 'Mulberries', which were towed across the Channel in sections before being assembled and sunk off the landing beaches at Omaha and Arromanches. These were designed to provide much improved facilities for the landing of supplies, but even these marvels of engineering ingenuity could not be expected to equal the tonnage capabilities and flexibility afforded by the facilities of a conventional port. This vital requirement, the early capture of a deep-water port in close proximity to the Allied bridgehead, is the subject of the events detailed in this volume of 'Battle Zone Normandy'.

The full story behind the planning and execution of Operation Neptune is covered in the six preceding volumes of this series and indeed the story has been examined in great detail in many other

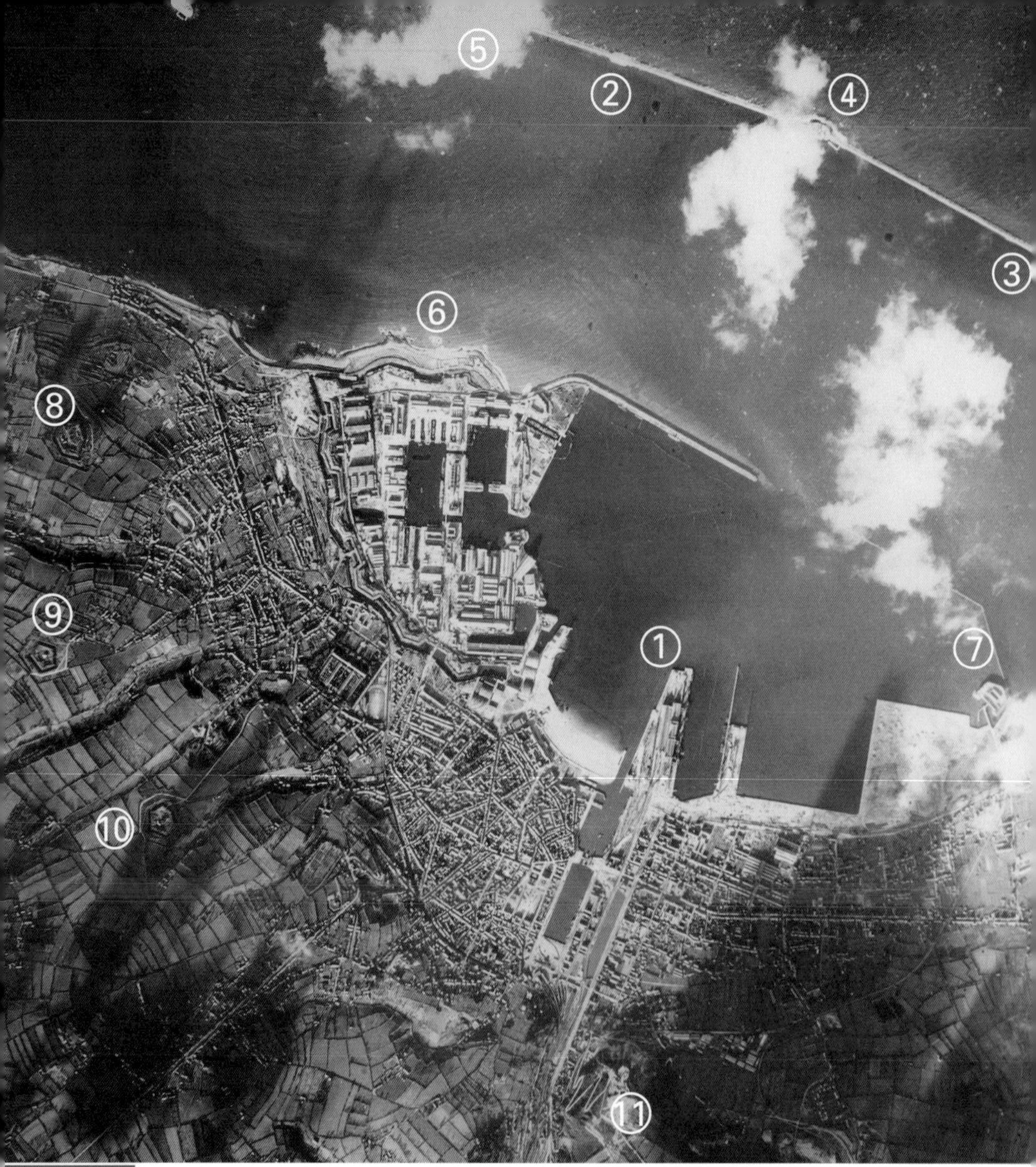

This aerial photograph of Cherbourg was taken shortly before the invasion. (1) The transatlantic liner terminal can be seen in the inner harbour. (2) The outer breakwater (the Digue Centrale) is visible, along with two of the forts built upon it: (3) the Fort de l'Est and (4) the Fort Central; (5) the Fort de l'Ouest (at the western end) is hidden by cloud. Another feature is (6) the naval arsenal, surrounded by its defensive wall, with five landward-facing bastions. The 1944 street grid can be seen but comparison with modern maps shows just how much Cherbourg has grown; (7) the Fort des Flamands, for example, now sits on reclaimed land. The intricate fields of the *bocage* cover the country around the city, and several pentagonal fortresses can be seen in the fields west of the city. These are (8) the Fort des Couplets (also known as the Fort Equeurdreville; *see pp. 79–80*), (9) the Fort du Tot and (10) the Fort des Fourches. Together with (11) the Fort du Roule these old French fortifications were integrated into the German defences that surrounded Cherbourg on the landward side. *(IWM CL16)*

Men from a combat engineer unit take respite from the war. Sitting in a doorway in a Cherbourg street they cook K rations over primus stoves on 28 June, with the sun finally shining down. *(USNA)*

works during the post-war period. By contrast, the battles that led to the successful seizure of the Norman port city of Cherbourg by the men of the United States Army's VII Corps have received little coverage. This book is therefore intended to shed some additional light on a neglected but fascinating aspect of the Normandy campaign and also to demonstrate exactly why the seizure of Cherbourg was so important. This account covers first the initial American move westwards across the Cotentin peninsula, seizing the initiative from the bridgeheads captured inland from the landing beach at Utah (the most westerly and northerly of the landing beaches). It explores how the Americans succeeded in cutting the Cotentin peninsula, thereby isolating the German defenders of Cherbourg and preventing their reinforcement from the southern, land route. (Cherbourg was effectively isolated from receiving any aid from either the air or the sea by virtue of the Allied control of the English Channel and overwhelming air superiority.) The book then looks at the subsequent American drive north, along three separate axes of advance, towards Cherbourg itself. It then details the bitter fighting in and around the town before exploring the fighting in the remainder of the Cotentin, after the surrender of Cherbourg by its garrison commander, *Generalleutnant* (GenLt) Karl-Wilhelm von Schlieben. Finally, this work will examine the first American attempt, by the US Army's VIII Corps, to drive south out of the Cotentin peninsula towards Coutances. While VIII Corps' advance ends this particular volume of 'Battle Zone Normandy' it links directly with two subsequent volumes, *Battle for St-Lô* and *Operation Cobra*.

CHAPTER 2

THE OPPOSING SIDES

Allied plans for Operation Overlord, the campaign to liberate German-occupied Western Europe, had several central provisions and the final decision to land along the Cotentin and Calvados coast was informed by many factors. The comparative proximity to the United Kingdom ensured that the Allies would be able to employ their impressive air forces in support of ground operations, while the beaches of the area were only lightly defended when compared to those of the Pas de Calais region (the area north of the Seine estuary), the other potential landing site. Another major consideration was the fact that the major port of Cherbourg, at the tip of the Cotentin, would be within striking distance from the landing beaches.

The capture of a major port was deemed vital in the initial Overlord and Neptune plans. Neptune had replaced a previous and less ambitious venture known as the COSSAC plan and envisaged amphibious landings by the Allies across five beaches from the mouth of the Orne River in the east to the Cotentin peninsula in the west. (COSSAC stood for Chief of Staff to the Supreme Allied Commander; this post was held by a Briton, Lieutenant-General F.E. Morgan.) One reason, among several, which resulted in this area being selected by the Allies, was the comparative proximity of a major port which could be used by the Allies. Under Neptune the First United States Army had as its top priority the 'capture of Cherbourg as quickly as possible'.

The considerable task of securing Cherbourg fell to First US Army's VII Corps under Major General (Maj Gen) Joseph Lawton Collins, nicknamed 'Lightning Joe' as a result of his

Private Fred Boone from Kentucky on the beach at Quinéville after the Americans had successfully forced their way into the town and beyond the formidable German defensive line based upon it. Boone is looking in the direction of the battles to come on the way to Cherbourg. To his right can be seen the extensive beach obstacles and a sign indicating that the beach is mined, both precautions taken in case the Allies landed here rather than further south. *(USNA)*

ruthless pursuit of Japanese forces in the fighting on Guadalcanal as commander of the 25th Infantry Division 'Tropic Lightning'. This determination to see his units press on and seize the advantage was to be very apparent as VII Corps moved to secure Cherbourg. Coming ashore across Utah Beach on 6 June and for several days afterwards, VII Corps was originally to have advanced towards Cherbourg directly in the aftermath of the invasion, but became bogged down by fierce German resistance.

General Collins, writing his autobiography after the war, remarked on his original hopes for the campaign.

'If Cherbourg could be seized quickly, it might not be necessary to seal off the peninsula in a time-consuming attack across its base'

Source: J.L. Collins, *Lightning Joe*, p. 203.

This ambition was to prove something of a pipe-dream as fierce German resistance, even in apparently impossible situations, prompted a change in US plans. Nevertheless, it offered 'Lightning Joe' the perfect opportunity to demonstrate that his nickname was just as applicable in the European theatre of operations as it had been in the Pacific.

US infantrymen using a pole charge, explosives attached to the end of long poles and thus delivered to the desired spot against enemy positions, to force access into fortifications. This procedure enabled the Americans to silence the guns of the lower levels of the formidable Fort du Roule at Cherbourg. *(USNA)*

The Cotentin peninsula

The Allied attack on Cherbourg was eventually to range across the length and breadth of the Cotentin peninsula, forcing the units of US VII Corps to fight in very diverse terrain. From the narrow *bocage* (hedgerow) country of the central and southern Cotentin to the less wooded north, and from the open country of the Cap de la Hague to the urban streets of Cherbourg, the men of VII Corps would be required to master all the terrain types they encountered. The Cotentin peninsula is in fact characterised by a wide variety of physical features, all of which would have a profound impact on the nature of the fighting that took place there. In the south the peninsula is cut by the River Douve and its

main tributary, the Merderet. These two rivers proved to be major obstacles to the American efforts to move west across the peninsula. While neither river was overly broad or swift-running, both flowed through low-lying and marshy terrain across which passage was slow at the best of times. The Germans, in seeking to maximise their defensive opportunities, destroyed the artificial drainage measures employed by the French, mainly a series of dams and locks, and in doing so flooded large areas of the southern Cotentin. This restricted movement substantially and meant that advances (and retreats) were canalised onto major arterial routes. As well as these low-lying rivers the Cotentin features many areas of water meadows with the undrained swampland of the *prairies marécageuses* at the base of the Cotentin peninsula between Carentan and St-Sauveur-de-Pierrepont further impeding access. This obstacle proved a particular problem when the US Army sought to move south after Cherbourg's fall.

An aerial photo of the Fort du Roule from the seaward side, taken on 8 July a few days after its capture by US forces. *(USNA)*

Into this equation must also be added the difficult and variable consideration of combat effectiveness. The American forces that fought in the northern Cotentin were a combination of tried and untried units. While the British forces, further east, experienced mixed results with some veteran units and more success with comparatively 'green' units, the US experience, at least so far as VII Corps was concerned, was the opposite. Generally speaking the newer US divisions, those without either a cadre of veterans or general combat experience, found the conditions in Normandy hard going, as will be seen. By contrast, previous fighting experience and, crucially, continuity of leadership either at the battalion, regimental or divisional level (or ideally all three) did appear to have an impact on units' willingness to advance and achieve objectives irrespective of the obstacles they faced (whether natural or German).

The hedgerow country of the northern Cotentin. The difficulty of moving vehicles through such narrow thoroughfares is all too apparent and the opportunities for ambush, in areas where the concept of a clearly delineated front-line was meaningless, were obviously legion. This view was taken looking south from Hill 158, an important feature overlooking Cherbourg's eastern defences. *(Author)*

THE GERMAN ARMY

The problems of terrain, of course, only become significant when they are being used to maximum advantage by a tenacious and skilled opponent. During the fighting for Cherbourg, the German forces ranged against VII Corps proved in large part to be worthy of this description. In June 1944, German forces in France came under the command of the *Oberbefehlshaber West* (Commander-in-Chief West), *Generalfeldmarschall* (Field Marshal) Gerd von

Rundstedt. In turn Rundstedt controlled two subordinate headquarters – *Heeresgruppe B* (Army Group B) and *Armee-Gruppe G* (Army Group G; despite its similar title in English, a lower-level headquarters than Army Group B). Army Group B was commanded by Field Marshal Erwin Rommel, and comprised the Fifteenth Army, deployed between the Dutch border and the Seine estuary with its main strength in the Pas de Calais, and the Seventh Army in Lower Normandy and Brittany. Army Group G was composed of First Army on the Atlantic coast south of Brittany, and Nineteenth Army in the south of France, along the Mediterranean coast. The Seventh Army, commanded by *Generaloberst* (Colonel-General) Friedrich Dollmann, was the force that was to meet the invaders head on during 6 June.

The Germans believed, prior to D-Day, that the main Allied attack would be in the Pas de Calais region. While German opinion was split on precisely where the main Allied effort would come, those who saw the Calais region as a likely landing site were reinforced in their belief by the machinations of Operation 'Fortitude'. This elaborate deception plan made skilful use of fake radio nets and imaginary armies; a whole US Army under Lieutenant General (Lt Gen) George S. Patton was 'stationed' in the Dover region opposite Calais to give further credence to the idea that the Allies would invade at this point.

The German Army was, by June 1944, seriously over-stretched. It was engaged in combat on two fronts, in the east against the vengeful might of Soviet Russia and in Italy against the Anglo-Americans. Until late 1943, therefore, the demands of the German forces in France and the Low Countries were not high on the priority list. Those resources that were directed west (and in the months leading up to the invasion far more were given to the German Army in France) often went to Fifteenth Army in the Pas de Calais, rather than to Seventh Army sitting in Normandy and Brittany. The much-vaunted Atlantic Wall of fortifications was strongest in the Calais area. By contrast, despite hard work in the weeks leading up to D-Day, on 6 June coastal defences in Lower Normandy were incomplete and lacking in depth.

The composition of the German Army in the west generally was also less impressive than in other theatres. Some units were second-rate, comprised of older or unfit German soldiers and increasingly, as the German position on the Eastern Front deteriorated and more and more troops were required, of unwilling supporters of the German cause. These *Hilfswilligen* or 'volunteers' frequently had not joined the German armed forces of their own free will; many were former prisoners-of-war taken from the Soviet forces. Their perceived unreliability in the fighting in the east necessitated their employment in the west, thus freeing up German troops for the Eastern Front.

A large group of Russians celebrate the German surrender in Cherbourg and with it their freedom. While many former Red Army prisoners of war had been press-ganged into fighting for the Germans it is unclear whether or not these men fall into this category. Their civilian clothes suggest they may have been employed by the Todt labour organisation, which built many of the defensive facilities in and around Cherbourg and across the northern Cotentin. *(USNA)*

The scale of employment of *Ost* units, literally 'east' troops, was considerable by June 1944. In May 1944, Seventh Army had amongst its units 23 battalions of *Ost* infantry. LXXXIV Corps, under the capable Russian Front veteran, *General der Artillerie* (General of Artillery) Erich Marcks, had (according to one source) a total strength of 42 rifle battalions, of which eight were *Osttruppen*. Before the fighting covered in this volume began, however, LXXXIV Corps was to lose its commanding officer, Marcks, killed by Allied aircraft on 12 June. This was a major blow for the German Army in Normandy. Marcks was neither the first nor the last senior German officer to pay the ultimate price for overwhelming Allied air superiority, 'death by fighter-bomber' as the Germans termed it. Ironically, Marcks had made frequent and increasingly desperate requests for a greater *Luftwaffe* (German Air Force) presence in the skies over Normandy. Marcks' replacement as temporary corps commander was *General der Artillerie* Wilhelm Fahrmbacher who moved over from XXV Corps until a permanent corps commander could be appointed.

LXXXIV Corps would be the main German formation involved in the fighting for Cherbourg and, on 6 June, three divisions of the corps occupied the northern Cotentin of which two, 243rd and 709th Infantry Divisions, were of the *Bodenständige* or 'static' type.

Despite its 'static' status, however, 243rd Infantry Division had progressively upgraded its mobility since its formation in July 1943. By May 1944 it was comparatively well equipped with mortars and a variety of Russian-built howitzers as well as mobile anti-aircraft defences. The division counted 11,529 men under command. Two of its three grenadier regiments comprised three battalions (the 920th Regiment had two), each equipped with around 45 machine guns and eight mortars. Each regiment also had a gun company equipped with six Russian 76.2-mm howitzers and an anti-tank company equipped with three 75-mm guns. All infantry battalions, with the exception of those of 920th Grenadier Regiment, were mounted on bicycles.

243rd Artillery Regiment had three battalions totalling ten batteries, with four guns per battery. The regiment's 1st and 2nd Battalions, each consisting of three batteries, were equipped with Russian 76.2-mm guns. The regiment's 3rd Battalion fielded three batteries of Russian-built 122-mm howitzers and a fourth manning 122-mm field pieces. 243rd Anti-Tank Battalion was equipped with 14 Marder 3s and 10 *Sturmgeschütz* IIIs. In addition, the battalion possessed a company of twelve 20-mm anti-aircraft guns, of which eight were on tracked chassis and the rest towed. 243rd Infantry Division also fielded 243rd Training and Replacement Battalion and a weak engineer battalion (243rd Engineer Battalion).

Also based in the northern Cotentin was 91st Airlanding Division, which was officially designated a reserve formation but joined LXXXIV Corps within hours of the invasion. It had a strength of between 7,000 and 8,000 men. This unit's commanding officer, GenLt Wilhelm Falley, was killed by US

German Units in the Battle for Cherbourg

LXXXIV Corps	***Gen der Art. Erich Marcks*** *(killed 12 June)*
	Gen der Art. Wilhelm Fahrmbacher *(relieved 18 June)*
	Gen der Inf. Dietrich von Choltitz *(from 18 June)*
Fortress Commander Cherbourg	***GenMaj Robert Sattler*** *(until 23 June)*
77th Infantry Division ***(77. Infanterie-Division)***	*GenLt Rudolf Stegmann (killed 17 June)*
1049th Grenadier Regiment *(Grenadier-Regiment 1049)*	*Oberst Rudolf Bacherer*
1050th Grenadier Regiment	*Oberst Brandt (captured 18 June)*
177th Artillery Regiment *(Artillerie-Regiment 177)*	*Oberst Stoltenburg*
177th Anti-Tank Battalion *(Panzerjäger-Abteilung 177)*	*Hauptmann Hiller*
177th Training and Replacement Btn *(Ausbildungs und Ersatz-Bataillon 177)*	*Hauptmann Burkhard*
177th Engineer Battalion *(Pionier-Bataillon 177)*	*Major Seifert*
91st Airlanding Division ***(91. Luftland-Division)***	*GenLt Wilhelm Falley (killed 6 June)*
	Oberst Eugen König (from 10 June)
1057th Grenadier Regiment	*Major von Saldern*
1058th Grenadier Regiment	*Oberst Beigang*
91st Fusilier Battalion *(Füsilier-Bataillon 352)*	
191st Artillery Regiment	*Oberstleutnant Kuhnert*
191st Anti-Tank Battalion	
191st Engineer Battalion	*Hauptmann Bonekamp*
243rd Infantry Division	*GenLt Heinz Hellmich (killed 17 June)*
920th Grenadier Regiment	*Oberst Bernhard Klosterkemper*
921st Grenadier Regiment	*Oberstleutnant Simon*
922nd Grenadier Regiment	*Oberstleutnant Franz Müller*
243rd Artillery Regiment	*Oberst Hellwig*
243rd Anti-Tank Battalion	*Major Bethke*
243rd Training and Replacement Btn	*Hauptmann Zwanzig*
243rd Engineer Battalion	*Hauptmann Reicherzer*
709th Infantry Division	*GenLt Karl-Wilhelm von Schlieben*
729th Grenadier Regiment	*Oberstleutnant Helmuth Rohrbach*
739th Grenadier Regiment	*Oberst Walther Köhn*
919th Grenadier Regiment	*Oberstleutnant Günther Keil*
561st *Ost* Battalion *(Ost-Bataillon 561)*	
649th *Ost* Battalion	*Hauptmann Gülker*
795th *Ost* Battalion	*Hauptmann Ziller*
1709th Artillery Regiment	*Oberst Reiter*
709th Anti-Tank Battalion	*Hauptmann Hümmerich*
709th Engineer Battalion	*Major Hornung*

Corps Units

Seventh Army Assault Battalion *(Sturm-Bataillon AOK 7)*	*Major Hugo Messerschmidt (KIA)*
Regimental Staff Seidel	*Oberstleutnant Seidel*
including 456th Heavy Artillery Battalion	*Oberstleutnant Fischer*
457th Heavy Artillery Battalion	*Hauptmann Schwarz*
(Artillerie-Regts. Stab z.b.V – schwere Artillerie-Abteilung 456, 457)	
101st Fortress Rocket Projector Regiment *(Stellungs-Werfer-Regiment 101)*	*Major Rasmer*
1261st Army Coastal Artillery Regiment *(Heeres-Küstenartillerie-Regiment 1261)*	*Oberst Gerhard Triepel*
1262nd Army Coastal Artillery Regiment	*Major Otte (died 15 June)*
260th Naval Artillery Detachment *(Marine-Artillerie-Abteilung 260)*	*Korvettenkäpitan Karl Weise*
30th Anti-Aircraft Artillery Regiment *(Heeres-Flakartillerie-Regimentstäbe 30)*	*Oberst Hermann*
17th Machine-Gun Battalion *(Maschinengewehr-Bataillon 17)*	*Major Reichert*
206th Panzer Battalion *(Panzer-Abteilung 206)*	
100th Panzer Training and Replacement Btn *(Panzer-Ausbildungs und Ersatz-Abteilung 100)*	*Major Bardenschlager*
101st Panzer Replacement Battalion *(Panzer-Ersatz-Abteilung 101)*	*Hauptmann Wenk*

Armoured vehicles used by the German forces in the Cherbourg battles were often adapted French designs like this old Renault R-35 tank, converted to carry a Czech 47-mm anti-tank gun, seen at Bittry on 20 June. Some of these vehicles served with 101st Panzer Replacement Battalion. *(USNA)*

paratroopers on D-Day itself. It comprised only two grenadier regiments, 1057th and 1058th. The division's 191st Artillery Regiment comprised three battalions, two of which suffered from being equipped, in large part, with 105-mm mountain guns, requiring ammunition that was not interchangeable with that of the standard German Army 105-mm field howitzer. 191st Anti-Tank Battalion was equipped with ten self-propelled and 39 motorised 75-mm anti-tank guns.

Within a short period of time, GenLt Rudolf Stegmann's 77th Infantry Division reinforced these units. This division was under-strength by *Wehrmacht* standards, numbering only 10,505 men in June 1944, including 1,410 *Hiwis* (Russians employed mainly in service roles). The division's 177th Artillery Regiment comprised just two battalions, fielding a total of sixteen 105-mm howitzers and twelve 88-mm anti-tank guns. While most of the division was eventually moved from its base near St-Malo, possibly as few as three battalions actually participated in the fighting in the northern Cotentin. Of these, two were sent to reinforce the German position north-west of Utah Beach, while the third was briefly attached to the fortress garrison at Cherbourg before being withdrawn to the south.

77th Infantry Division comprised only two grenadier regiments instead of the usual three. 1049th Grenadier Regiment had three battalions, each with 40 machine guns and eight 81-mm mortars. 1050th Grenadier Regiment's three battalions each fielded 40 machine guns and seven 81-mm mortars. Both regiments possessed a company equipped with three heavy anti-tank guns; 1049th Grenadier Regiment also had six Russian infantry guns, while 1050th Grenadier Regiment had just two. 177th Anti-Tank Battalion comprised two companies, one with twelve 50-mm and the other with twelve 75-mm anti-tank guns. Of these weapons, six of the 50-mm guns were static and the remainder motorized.

The men of GenLt Karl-Wilhelm von Schlieben's 709th Infantry Division, charged with holding Cherbourg and manning bunkers and other fortifications in the eastern Cotentin, averaged around 30 years of age. For the purposes of operations based around good defensive positions this was more than adequate, as the American forces would soon discover *en route* to Cherbourg.

709th Infantry Division's strength at 1 June 1944 was 12,320 men. The division's 729th Grenadier Regiment, with all companies mounted on bicycles, comprised three battalions, each equipped

By June 1944 the Germans were building facilities for their flying bombs and rockets in the Cotentin peninsula. This is the V-2 rocket site at Sottevast, 10 km south of Cherbourg. Designed as a storage, servicing and launch facility, Sottevast was still incomplete when overrun by US forces. *(USNA)*

with 46 machine guns and four mortars. 739th Grenadier Regiment, comprising only two battalions, each equipped with 48 machine guns, fielded only one bicycle-mounted company in each of its battalions. 919th Grenadier Regiment had three battalions, each fielding one bicycle-mounted company and equipped with 50 machine guns, four flame-throwers and eight mortars. In addition, all three grenadier regiments possessed an anti-tank company with six 75-mm and three 50-mm guns. 919th Grenadier Regiment also had an additional company with six Russian howitzers and a further anti-tank company with static pieces. 649th *Ost* Battalion was equipped with 46 machine guns and 1 mortars, while 561st *Ost* Battalion possessed nine mortars and some 4.5-inch anti-tank weapons. 795th *Ost* Battalion counted 44 machine guns and 15 mortars among its armament.

709th Infantry Division fielded a total of 11 batteries of artillery. Two batteries were each equipped with four Czech-built 100-mm howitzers; three batteries fielded four French 105-mm guns each; three batteries were each equipped with four French

155-mm howitzers; and three batteries possessed four Russian 76.2-mm guns each. 709th Anti-Tank Battalion had nine 75-mm Pak 40 guns mounted on tracked chassis, plus 12 towed Pak 40s and nine 37-mm anti-aircraft guns.

A rather curious scene in Montebourg, 21 June. Here the two worlds of the military and the civilian in Normandy come together in all their stark disparity. As US engineers move cautiously along the street, with a mine detector apparently in action, they are passed by French civilians hauling a cart – far more likely to set off any mines than individuals on foot. *(USNA)*

There were a number of independent units also available to LXXXIV Corps. *Major* Hugo Messerschmidt's Seventh Army Assault Battalion fielded three infantry companies and one heavy company with machine guns and howitzers, plus an artillery company and attached engineer units. 456th and 457th Heavy Artillery Battalions (Motorised) were equipped identically, each with four 122-mm guns and eight 152-mm howitzers. 101st Fortress Rocket Projector Regiment had three battalions, with 54 six-barrelled *Nebelwerfer* launchers in total. 17th Machine-Gun Battalion counted three companies, each with 12 machine guns, and an anti-tank platoon with 50-mm guns. 902nd Assault Gun Battalion fielded Sturmgeschütz III assault guns, while 206th Panzer Battalion was equipped with French Hotchkiss and Somua tanks and based west of Cherbourg prior to D-Day.

While it rapidly became obvious to the German high command that Cherbourg was a target for the US Army as it moved out of the Utah beachhead, the exact route and method the Americans would use were still unknown. As late as 11 June German Seventh Army believed that the US airborne forces, fighting as infantry, would be withdrawn from the battles around Ste-Mère-Église and 'recommitted by air in the expected major attack against Cherbourg'. German intelligence considered this a more likely avenue of US attack than the push across the Cotentin to cut the peninsula, although this too was considered possible. At this time the Germans believed that an Allied amphibious landing on the west coast of the Cotentin in the bay of Vauville (south of Cap de la Hague) to facilitate the seizure of Cherbourg was also a distinct possibility. While the Germans frequently proved adept at anticipating Allied activities and strengths, it is perhaps worth noting that on 15 June Seventh Army judged that the Allies had some 25 divisions in Normandy, a considerable overestimate.

FESTUNG CHERBOURG

Cherbourg, as a major port on the Channel coast, had been extensively fortified to guard against any efforts to seize it from the seaward direction. The Germans, using many existing French fortifications, embarked on a major programme of fort- and bunker-building across the length and breadth of the Cotentin in the months leading up to the Allied invasion. A great many

The Fort de l'Est on the outer breakwater of Cherbourg's Grande Rade was used as part of the port's defences by the Germans. *(Jonathan Falconer)*

German positions remain to this day and several are visited in the various tours described later in this volume. Even a cursory walk in and around the Cherbourg area will reveal innumerable blockhouses and strongpoints of Second World War vintage. Although a major demolition programme during the 1950s removed many, those that remain are indicative of how well defended, in static terms, the port and its environs were. While the Allies never seriously considered the seaward approaches to Cherbourg as a means to secure the port, due to the dangers the defences posed, the landward route, or *Landfront* in German, was likely also to be difficult.

An American soldier stands in a ruined building in the centre of Cherbourg. In front of him are stacks of what looks like German 88-mm ammunition – ammunition that was not used in the fighting. (*USNA*)

The problems of taking Cherbourg overland had been demonstrated starkly in 1940. During the Battle of France and subsequent evacuation of British and French personnel, troops of the British Expeditionary Force moved through Cherbourg. The British managed to hold the town with a force that numbered little more than a brigade through skilful use of the undulating terrain and the existing French defensive positions. On the German side adequate preparation of this avenue of attack should therefore have been afforded high priority. However, until November 1943 the focus of the Cherbourg defences was still centred on a likely Allied effort from the sea. Defences on the landward side of the town had been comparatively overlooked.

In November 1943 Field Marshal Rommel instructed that the Cherbourg garrison's ability to defend against an attack from the south should be strengthened significantly. These preparations incorporated many of the innovations later seen elsewhere in Normandy such as the erection of upright posts, known colloquially as *Rommelsspargel* or 'Rommel's asparagus' and designed to prevent glider landings, plus the digging of anti-tank ditches and the laying of minefields and bunker-building by the Todt labour organisation.

Major Hopf, on the staff of *Generalmajor* (GenMaj) Robert Sattler (then commanding 'Fortress Cherbourg'), noted the arrival of a variety of senior German commanders in the six months that preceded the Allied invasion of Normandy. The list of luminaries reads like a 'Who's Who' of the German Army: 13 January, *General der Artillerie* Alfred Jodl (chief of Hitler's military staff); 30 January, GenMaj (as he then was) von Schlieben; 30 January, Field Marshal Rommel; 4 March, Col-Gen Dollmann and so on. While such efforts were likely to have borne fruit in the longer term, German exercises conducted in the weeks before D-Day showed that much work was still to be done. In a series of exercises, GenMaj von Schlieben, later the commandant of the Cherbourg garrison, succeeded in capturing

A resigned GenMaj Sattler in American captivity, 29 June 1944. Sattler was the original commanding officer of the Cherbourg garrison before becoming GenLt von Schlieben's deputy. Sattler's smart attire contrasts sharply with the bedraggled, grimy uniforms of most of the surrendered German personnel in Cherbourg. (*USNA*)

the port by breaking through the defences south of the town. This was a source of concern for the Seventh Army command but, lacking men and resources across the whole area of its responsibility, it could do little to redress such problems.

The American position after D-Day

On 6 June the Americans landed at Omaha Beach and at Utah Beach, on the right flank of the Allied front. These landing sites were on either side of the River Vire estuary, which also formed the confluence of three other rivers. At the head of the estuary lay the important town and road junction of Carentan. The capture of this town was achieved only after a bloody and prolonged engagement involving American airborne forces, parachuted in during the early hours of 6 June with very mixed success, many units being scattered kilometres from their intended objectives. At Carentan, however, sufficient American forces were in place to attempt to seize the town. In a straight match between airborne units – on the one side were the paratroopers of the US 101st Airborne Division, the 'Screaming Eagles' and on the other the equally tenacious soldiers of the German 6th Paratroop Regiment – the Americans managed finally to prevail. After heavy fighting that lasted roughly from 8 to 15 June Carentan was finally secured by the Americans.

The capture of this town was highly significant as it meant that the two American bridgeheads were now linked together for the first time. With an American drive towards Cherbourg along the north-westerly axis from the bridgehead at Utah having been frustrated by bitter German resistance, the decision was taken to move due west instead, splitting German forces in the Cotentin peninsula into two and isolating Cherbourg in the process. In order to cut the Cotentin peninsula, the Americans needed to secure a bridgehead on the west bank of the River Merderet. The likely site was approximately 3 km west of Ste-Mère-Église at la Fière. In fierce fighting, reminiscent of that to the south at Carentan, American paratroopers, this time of 82nd Airborne Division, forced their way across to establish the effective jumping-off point for the American push west.

However, even a casual glance at the map of the Cotentin peninsula is sufficient to show that the logical direction for an American drive on Cherbourg from their landing areas east of Ste-Mère-Église would be to push north-west. American progress, though, was blocked in this sector by formidable German defensive arrangements along a ridgeline that stretched from the small coastal town of Quinéville and ran south-west and inland to Montebourg and then to le Ham. Attacks towards this defensive line proved that it would be difficult to push through along this, the most direct route to Cherbourg. This line had been identified by von Schlieben as the key position in front of Cherbourg. If it should collapse then the preferred American route to the port city, north-west through Valognes and along the Cherbourg–Valognes highway, would lie open.

US engineers clearing rubble and wreckage in Valognes, 24 June. Getting roads and other communications working again was essential to continuing the Allied advance. *(USNA)*

The German defenders, although a mixed bag of forces from 709th, 243rd and 91st Divisions, plus men from the Seventh Army's Assault Battalion, occupied well-sited defensive positions. The Seventh Army Assault Battalion, while among the best-equipped and trained units that Seventh Army had available in Normandy, had suffered heavy casualties after repeated counter-attacks against American paratroopers in the Ste-Mère-Église area during the days immediately after the invasion. While still retaining an impressive cohesion, its combat power was waning. The Seventh Army war diary noted on 10 June that, 'our own troops have fought well, particularly the Seventh Army High Command Assault Battalion', but maintaining this level of combat effectiveness was proving increasingly difficult. The defenders also possessed a generous allocation of artillery pieces from the three battalions of 243rd Artillery Regiment, 456th and 457th (Motorised) Artillery Battalions, various individual guns and at least two coastal batteries. The principal caveats to this strength in material were a lack of ammunition and the constant harassment that the German gunners faced from Allied air attacks and naval gunfire support from Allied warships. Even so, the Germans managed to stabilise the position north of Utah through the transfer of elements of the comparatively weak 77th Infantry Division (under strength and ill-equipped, especially in artillery) from Brittany to positions south-east of Valognes. However, as the Germans understood only too well, securing the defences in one sector meant weakening their position elsewhere.

Despite its overwhelming numerical superiority in terms of weapons and vehicles, the US Army still found it necessary to improvise from time to time. Here horse-drawn carts are used to bring up supplies through the streets of Montebourg, 21 June. *(USNA)*

By 14 June continuous pressure by 4th Infantry Division, a heavily reinforced unit which had come ashore at Utah Beach on 6 June, had forced the Germans back. The Americans had finally managed to seize the German defences based on the Quinéville ridgeline to the east and west of the town of Montebourg. Montebourg, however, remained in German hands. The positions now occupied by the US forces were still only those that had been originally set as objectives for D-Day itself. The original intention, as laid down in the Revised VII Corps Field Order of 28 May, anticipated a direct advance on Cherbourg, from Utah, along the Valognes axis. No mention was made at that time of any intent to sever the Cotentin, although intelligence on additional German forces in the area did prompt a revision of the time it would take to secure Cherbourg to D+15 days.

However, the difficulties encountered by 4th Infantry Division in the fighting north of Utah had already obliged the First Army commander, Lt Gen Omar Bradley, to change the dictates of the Neptune plan in the face of fierce and only slowly yielding German resistance. On 9 June Bradley decided that, while 4th Infantry Division continued its push towards Montebourg, additional US forces should first drive westwards to the far side of the Cotentin peninsula, swinging around the German positions based on Montebourg in a south-westerly arc, before beginning an advance towards Cherbourg itself. The unspoken hope of this plan was that outflanking the Montebourg positions might also prompt a German withdrawal in the face of being cut off entirely from Cherbourg.

The Germans were very fortunate, during the early days of the campaign, to secure a copy of the Neptune plan. This was captured on the body of a dead American officer found in an abandoned landing craft. Interestingly, the German Seventh Army war diary claimed that much of the information disclosed in this document was not fundamentally new; in fact that 'the views of the [German Seventh] Army as to the enemy's tactical intention were confirmed by capture of the plans of operations of the VII American Army Corps'. The Germans were therefore not surprised to see that VII Corps had as its principal objective the port of Cherbourg.

The drive westwards was contingent on being able to move out of the small bridgeheads established on the River Merderet on 8/9 June. The seizure of these operationally vital areas had been achieved through determined and concerted action by US paratroopers and not a little good fortune as well. Isolated groups of paratroopers from 82nd Airborne Division had been fighting on the west bank of the Merderet, and west of the town of Ste-Mère-Église since the early hours of 6 June. The efforts of two men from 2nd Battalion, 507th Parachute Infantry Regiment (PIR), to find a way back eastwards towards the main American position led to the discovery of a submerged but usable road across the Merderet north of the small hamlet of la Fière. This find was exploited, at some considerable cost, and eventually resulted in the la Fière bridgehead from where the main thrust to sever the Cotentin would begin.

The original Neptune plan had envisaged 90th Infantry Division being committed on the right flank of 4th Infantry Division for the projected drive north up the Cotentin peninsula. Now, with the decision having been taken for the drive across the peninsula, 90th Division was ordered to take over from elements of 82nd Airborne Division and move to the west from the bridgehead at la Fière and at Chef-du-Pont, approximately 1 km further south. 90th Infantry Division's initial progress in this vital attack was unimpressive and was to have serious ramifications.

CHAPTER 3

CUTTING THE COTENTIN PENINSULA

The American decision to drive across the peninsula was designed to facilitate the capture of Cherbourg by outflanking positions of German strength and also, according to VII Corps records, to 'prevent the arrival of any additional reinforcement of the Cherbourg defenders and likewise to forestall any orderly withdrawal of troops from the Cherbourg area'. Before any useful advance could be made, however, Maj Gen Collins decided to 'clean house' in his corps, to employ a particularly apt American euphemism. The combat effectiveness of 90th Infantry Division had been called into question on several occasions during the fighting to move beyond the Merderet bridgehead and Collins himself had personally seen men of 90th Infantry Division hiding in ditches in the vicinity of la Fière. Collins thought that 'it was obvious they were malingering' and endeavoured to do something about it. In his autobiography, *Lightning Joe*, written at the end of a long and varied post-war career, Collins claimed that he tried to inspire these soldiers to fight by recounting tales of 90th Infantry Division's successes in France in 1918 but all to no avail. 90th Infantry Division's commander since mid-January 1944, Brigadier General (Brig Gen) Jay W. MacKelvie, was removed from command, but with the American official history stressing that MacKelvie was 'relieved without prejudice'.

Other assessments of this problem stressed that such concerns as were apparent could probably be traced back to the period immediately prior to MacKelvie taking over. MacKelvie had served earlier as the Divisional Artillery Commander. Eisenhower believed that these shortcomings in combat could be attributed to the fact that the division 'had not been properly brought up'. Two regimental commanders were also replaced at this time. Brig Gen MacKelvie's successor as divisional commander was Maj Gen Eugene Landrum, who had been the deputy commander of US VII Corps until this point. It is perhaps worth noting that Maj Gen Landrum himself was relieved of command in early July 1944 when, once again, 90th Infantry Division made little or no progress, this time during the American break-out to the south of the Cotentin. In fact the 90th Division remained a problem until Maj Gen Ray McLain took over command.

(L to R) General Eisenhower, Lt Gen Bradley and Maj Gen Collins. *(USNA)*

Order of Battle US Army VII Corps
Cherbourg Campaign, June 1944

Commanding General	**Maj Gen Joseph Lawton Collins**
Deputy Corps Commander	*Maj Gen Eugene Landrum*

4th Infantry Division, The 'Ivy' Division, 12 June 1944

Commanding General	*Maj Gen Raymond O. Barton*
Assistant Divisional Commander	*Brig Gen Henry Barber*
Artillery Commander	*Brig Gen Harold W. Blakeley*

Organic Units

8th Infantry Regiment	*Col James Van Fleet*
12th Infantry Regiment	*Col James S. Luckett*
22nd Infantry Regiment	*Col Hervey A. Tribolet*

4th Reconnaissance Troop; 4th Engineer Combat Battalion;
20th Field Artillery Battalion (155-mm howitzer);
29th, 42nd, 44th Field Artillery Battalions (105-mm howitzer)

Attached Units

Task Force Barber (6th Armored Group);
70th Tank Battalion (minus C Company);
39th Infantry Regt (from 9th Infantry Division);
A and C Companies, 899th Tank Destroyer Battalion (Self-Propelled)

9th Infantry Division, 'Hitler's Nemesis', 14 June 1944

Commanding General	*Maj Gen Manton S. Eddy*
Assistant Divisional Commander	*Brig Gen Donald A. Stroh*
Artillery Commander	*Brig Gen Reese M. Howell*

Organic Units

39th Infantry Regiment	*Col Harry A. Flint*
47th Infantry Regiment	*Col George W. Smythe*
60th Infantry Regiment	*Col Frederick J. de Rohan*

9th Reconnaissance Troop; 15th Engineer Combat Battalion;
34th Field Artillery Battalion (155-mm howitzer);
26th, 60th, 84th Field Artillery Battalions (105-mm howitzer)

Attached Units

746th Tank Battalion (minus A Company)

Detached Units

39th Infantry Regiment (to 4th Infantry Division)

This episode served as a timely reminder of several important considerations that underpinned all the various operations to seize Cherbourg. First, that the enemy would not be dislodged easily and that offensive action was the only solution. German troops to date had fought on even when individual unit positions

79th Infantry Division, 'Cross of Lorraine' Division, 19 June 1944

Commanding General	*Maj Gen Ira T. Wyche*
Assistant Divisional Commander	*Brig Gen Frank U. Greer*
Artillery Commander	*Brig Gen George D. Wahl*
Organic Units	
313th Infantry Regiment	*Col Sterling A. Wood*
314th Infantry Regiment	*Col Warren A. Robinson*
315th Infantry Regiment	*Col Porter B. Wiggins*

79th Reconnaissance Troop, 304th Engineer Combat Battalion;
312th Field Artillery Battalion (155-mm howitzer);
310th, 311th, 904th Field Artillery Battalions (105mm howitzer)

82nd Airborne Division 'All American', 12 June 1944

Commanding Officer	*Maj Gen Matthew B. Ridgway*
Assistant Divisional Commander:	*Brig Gen James M. Gavin*
Artillery Commander	*Col Francis A. March*
Organic Units	
505th Parachute Infantry Regiment	*Lt Col William E. Ekman*
507th Parachute Infantry Regiment	*Col George V. Millett, Jr.*
508th Parachute Infantry Regiment	*Col Roy Lindquist*
325th Glider Infantry Regiment	*Col Harry L. Lewis*

307th Airborne Engineer Btn; 80th Airborne AA Artillery Btn;
319th Glider Field Artillery Btn; 320th Glider Field Artillery Btn;
376th Parachute Field Artillery Btn; 456th Parachute Field Artillery Btn

Attached Units

2nd Btn, 401st Glider Infantry Regiment (from 101st Airborne Division)

90th Infantry Division 'Tough Ombres', 12 June 1944

Commanding Officer	*Brig Gen Jay W. MacKelvie*
Assistant Divisional Commander	*Brig Gen Samuel P. Williams*
Artillery Commander	*Brig Gen John M. Devine*
Organic Units	
357th Infantry Regiment	*Col Philip H. Ginder*
358th Infantry Regiment	*Col James V. Thompson*
359th Infantry Regiment	*Col Clarke K. Fales*

90th Reconnaissance Troop; 325th Engineer Combat Battalion;
343rd, 344th, 345th, 915th Field Artillery Battalions (105-mm howitzer)

Attached Units

746th Tank Battalion

were clearly untenable. Any failure by US forces to push hard in the fighting for Cherbourg would result in delays and precious time gained for the Germans to demolish the port. With the future of the Allied lodgement in Normandy still appearing reliant on Cherbourg's quick capture, delays in securing it could not be allowed. Second, this incident also demonstrated that Collins, as corps commander, was unlikely to be satisfied with second-best and experience in combat had to be gained quickly with lessons learned and solutions to problems implemented immediately.

This was not an auspicious beginning for VII Corps' key mission, to sever the Cotentin and secure Cherbourg. As a result of this change in leadership, and lingering general concerns about its potential performance in heavy combat, 90th Infantry Division was replaced in the central role in the American advance westwards. The drive to the east coast of the Cotentin was now to be spearheaded by the more reliable 9th Infantry Division under Maj Gen Manton S. Eddy. In contrast to the 90th, 9th Infantry Division had enjoyed a far greater degree of continuity of command, with its commanding officer, Eddy, having led it through the campaigns in North Africa from late 1942 and in Sicily in 1943. (Eddy was later promoted to 3-star rank and commanded XII Corps in Patton's Third Army.) The advance elements of 9th Infantry Division had only landed in France on 10 June and were committed to battle on 14 June.

Alongside 9th Infantry Division was the well-proven but under-strength 82nd Airborne Division. Again, the fighting spirit of the airborne troops was not in doubt but it should be remembered also that the parachute and glider units were light formations, trained and equipped for specific operations in advance of the main Allied forces. The 82nd had been in almost constant contact with the enemy since the early hours of 6 June and its mission had been expected to end within days if not hours of the successful Allied landings on the Normandy coast.

In the coming drive, both divisions elected to employ only two of their three regiments, maintaining a third in reserve. Maj Gen Collins' plan to cut the peninsula called for the 82nd to attack in the southern area of the American bridgehead from la Fière along an axis that described the Pont l'Abbé–St-Sauveur-le-Vicomte road. 9th Infantry Division was tasked with an attack towards Ste-Colombe while the out-of-favour 90th Infantry Division was assigned objectives along the north flank of the American push.

On 14 June the American attack started in the south, with 358th Infantry Regiment pushing forward to a point west of Pont l'Abbé. Units of 82nd Airborne Division made good initial progress, starting from a noon attack, with 325th Glider Infantry

Regiment (GIR) to the left or south of the Pont l'Abbé–St-Sauveur-le-Vicomte road and 507th PIR to the north. The 507th's progress suffered slightly in the face of a determined German counter-attack but it still achieved an advance of a couple of kilometres by nightfall. At this juncture 358th Infantry Regiment was relieved by the 359th (also of 90th Infantry Division) and this unit turned north towards Gottot where 60th Infantry Regiment from 9th Infantry Division was facing stiff enemy resistance. Only after a slow and ponderous advance under German fire did units reach the road west of Gottot.

A technician 5th grade operates a radio near Étienville (Pont l'Abbé), 21 June. *(USNA)*

US troops use a German truck at St-Sauveur-le-Vicomte, 19 June. *(USNA)*

To the north, 90th Infantry Division was once again experiencing difficulties, taking two days to secure the village of Gourbesville no more than 4 km to the north-west of la Fière. The American official history is reasonably even-handed about the continuing problems of this unit. While claiming that the division was suffering from virtual paralysis at this point, it also pointed out that 'there is no question that the German defence on the north and north-west was substantially stronger than on the west'. While Maj Gen Landrum faced elements of the recently arrived German 77th Infantry Division, opposition to the drive due west was still only from 91st Airlanding Division, now beaten down to battle-weary *Kampfgruppen* (battle groups). Nevertheless, the performance of the 90th was still a cause for concern.

15 June saw the tempo of the American advance increase substantially. This was particularly evident within 82nd Airborne Division's area of operations which saw, in particular, 325th GIR advancing to within a short distance of the comparatively substantial town of St-Sauveur-le-Vicomte, which sits astride the River Douve. To the north of this position 60th Infantry Regiment, by contrast, faced a strong, tank-supported counter-attack which succeeded in driving the Americans all the way back

to their original jumping-off point. Additional fighting saw the 60th recover some of its gains. By reorganising the axis of advance of some of their units the Americans contrived to introduce an additional infantry regiment, the 47th, into the gap between 60th Infantry Regiment (under Colonel Frederick de Rohan) and the 359th. 47th Infantry Regiment (under Colonel George W. Smythe) moved rapidly towards the high ground west of the small town of Orglandes, which it reached by nightfall on 15 June.

Troops of 82nd Airborne Division in St-Sauveur-le-Vicomte, 16 June. *(USNA)*

The next day, 16 June, Collins planned to encourage his units to move with all speed towards the River Douve and instructed 325th GIR, the most southerly unit of the American advance, to push on regardless of whether other formations to the north were making similar progress. Reaching the river with all haste was vital, as Collins saw it, to prevent the Germans establishing a defensive line along it. The 'main effort' of VII Corps, Collins declared, was 'now to cut the peninsula'. While this decision was not without risk, as the parachute and glider infantry units were lightly armed, Collins' determination to maintain momentum and continue to keep the pressure on the hard-hit German forces was, in the circumstances, correct. Contemporary intelligence reports, gleaned from VII Corps HQ records, note that the German forces were being steadily reduced in the bitter fighting and that

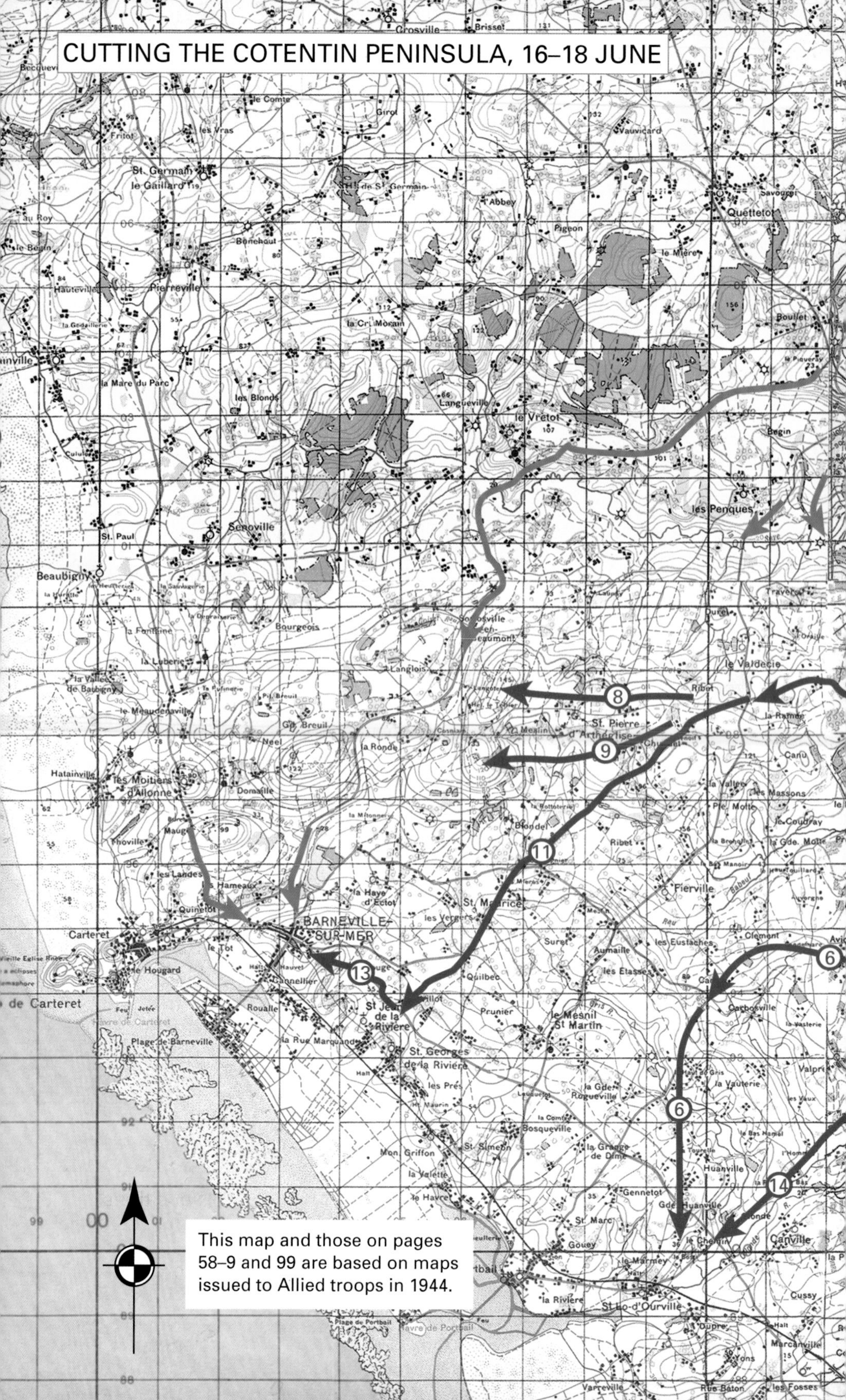
CUTTING THE COTENTIN PENINSULA, 16–18 JUNE
This map and those on pages 58–9 and 99 are based on maps issued to Allied troops in 1944.

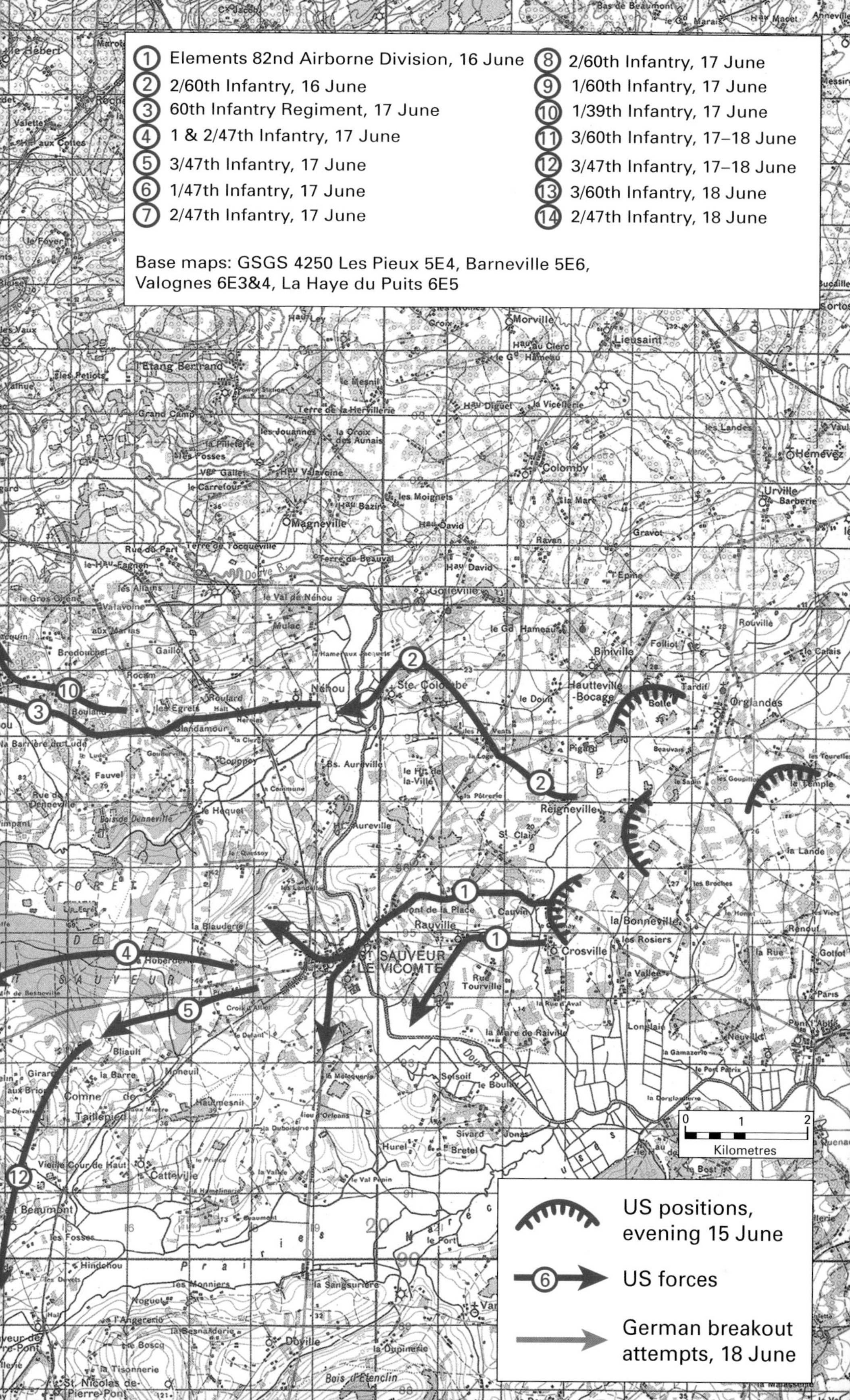

1 Elements 82nd Airborne Division, 16 June
2 2/60th Infantry, 16 June
3 60th Infantry Regiment, 17 June
4 1 & 2/47th Infantry, 17 June
5 3/47th Infantry, 17 June
6 1/47th Infantry, 17 June
7 2/47th Infantry, 17 June
8 2/60th Infantry, 17 June
9 1/60th Infantry, 17 June
10 1/39th Infantry, 17 June
11 3/60th Infantry, 17–18 June
12 3/47th Infantry, 17–18 June
13 3/60th Infantry, 18 June
14 2/47th Infantry, 18 June
Base maps: GSGS 4250 Les Pieux 5E4, Barneville 5E6, Valognes 6E3&4, La Haye du Puits 6E5
St. Sauveur Le Vicomte
0 1 2
Kilometres
US positions, evening 15 June
US forces
German breakout attempts, 18 June

In the ruins of St-Sauveur-le-Vicomte, men of 505th Parachute Infantry Regiment of 82nd Airborne Division regroup and rearm following the heavy and bloody fighting to secure this important town. This picture also shows the commanding officer of 2nd Battalion, 505th PIR, Lt Col Benjamin Vandervoort, complete with a broken leg and crutches that did little to impede his leadership. John Wayne famously played Vandervoort in the film *The Longest Day*. (*USNA*)

continued pressure, in the form of more direct thrusts, was likely to strain German command and control to breaking point. VII Corps HQ considered that 'a complete breakdown of [German] supply appeared impending'. Once again, Lightning Joe was living up to his reputation and taking the fight to the enemy. Rapid re-structuring ensured that US forces were again re-configured to reflect the area of main effort, with 39th Infantry Regiment rejoining 9th Infantry Division. The division also benefited from the attachment of 359th Infantry Regiment, from 90th Division, meaning that it now fielded four infantry regiments in its role as the corps' spearhead.

As on the previous day, 16 June saw 82nd Airborne Division also achieve rapid progress with both 505th PIR and 325th GIR reaching a point east of St-Sauveur-le-Vicomte by midday. Here they were reinforced by 508th PIR from its reserve position.

Quick thinking by Maj Gen Matthew B. Ridgway, the dynamic commanding officer of the 82nd, enabled his division to grab a vital position across the River Douve. After seeing German forces engaged in a temporary, tactical retreat through the town, Ridgway urged his lightly equipped paratroops to rush forward and cross the river, thereby establishing a bridgehead on the western side of the town before the German defenders had time to organise any meaningful defence.

American wounded being cared for by US medics on 21 June. To the left of the vehicle, a captured German transport employed in a new role, is a makeshift dressing station in a Norman farmhouse. These soldiers were wounded during American efforts to secure a bridgehead across the River Douve. *(USNA)*

At corps level, Maj Gen Collins, too, was still urging 9th Infantry Division to push ahead to the Douve line and to disregard the previously identified interim objectives if the opportunity presented itself. Maj Gen Eddy was instructed to push 47th and 60th Infantry Regiments on to the Douve and to deploy 39th Infantry Regiment to protect his northern flank. The 47th was instructed to seize the high ground east of Ste-Colombe and managed to do so, but only after a 'hard fight' in the vicinity of Biniville, the location of the last high ground east of the river.

Still further to the west 2nd Battalion, 60th Infantry Regiment, made even more dramatic progress. Supported by part of 746th

Two US infantrymen prepare to fire rifle grenades into buildings occupied by German snipers, 27 June. (*USNA*)

Tank Battalion, 2nd Battalion, 60th Infantry Regiment (2/60th Infantry) entered the town of Ste-Colombe and crossed the River Douve where it splits into three streams between Ste-Colombe and Néhou. The Americans managed to seize a small bridgehead west of the river before being reinforced by 3/60th Infantry during the night.

The Germans, of course, were not idle during this time and were, if anything, better-trained and more experienced than their opponents in grasping at every chance presented to them during the course of the fighting. While US pressure in the Montebourg area continued along with the rapid American progress west across the peninsula, German Seventh Army was considering how best to respond. On 14 June it was decided that German forces on the northern front of the Cotentin should be split into two battle groups. The first, under GenLt von Schlieben, was named Battle Group *von Schlieben* and comprised all those troops along and north of the Montebourg line, predominantly 709th Division and part of 243rd and 77th Divisions. This group was to prepare to fall back into Cherbourg if necessary.

The second was Battle Group *Hellmich* (commanded by GenLt Heinz Hellmich), comprising elements of 243rd, 77th and 91st

Divisions west and south of the River Merderet. This group, it was mooted, would fall back and re-deploy to the area west of St-Sauveur-le-Vicomte and from there to a line north of la Haye-du-Puits. The situation of this second German battle group was precarious. Seventh Army's war diary described it in the following terms: 'hard-pressed by the complete breakdown of the supply system and by the enemy's extraordinary superiority in material. Holding position in this sector is only a question of hours.' In fact, a better illustration of the precarious position of German forces in the Cotentin is also to be found in Seventh Army's war diary, which stated that the main reason to release 77th Infantry Division (and other units) to the south was for no other reason than that 'Cherbourg has not enough ammunition and food for the intended number of troops'. All artillery capable of employment in mobile warfare was also to be 'sent to the south to avoid being lost'.

A modern view of the first of the three crucial bridges that span the River Douve and its minor tributaries at Ste-Colombe, looking west, the direction of the advance of 2nd Battalion, 60th Infantry Regiment. As can be seen in the picture, the first bridge is on the western outskirts of the village. *(Author)*

Confusion between Hitler's headquarters, Seventh Army's HQ and Rommel's own HQ meant that little happened for several days after 14 June save for a number of contradictory orders being issued to the two beleaguered formations. Eventually, on 16 June, Seventh Army instructed 77th Infantry Division to disengage. According to Seventh Army's war diary the intention was 'to employ only the 709th Infantry Division and parts of the

243rd Infantry Division to defend the inner belt of the fortress and to release 77th Infantry Division to the south.' Hours later this order was countermanded and 77th Infantry Division instead instructed that it was to stay where it was. Eventually, on 17 June, GenLt von Schlieben was informed that his men could withdraw into Cherbourg and at 1030 hours that day Seventh Army received the following message from Hitler, *via* Army Group West:

> 'Fortress Cherbourg must be held at all costs. Delaying action by the northern group at Fortress Cherbourg must be maintained, in order to retard the progress of the enemy. A complete evacuation is not authorised. The possession of Cherbourg is decisive.'
>
> *Source:* Seventh Army war diary, entry for 17 June 1944; RG 407, Box 24154, Folder 488, US National Archives.

The remains of a *Luftwaffe* bunker near the summit of Hill 145. *(Author)*

Despite Hitler's order, a day later those elements of 77th Infantry Division caught north of the American advance attempted, finally, to move south. While the Germans delayed, further south the fate of Cherbourg was being decided. The US 9th Infantry Division's 60th and 47th Infantry Regiments moved westwards to cut the Cotentin peninsula. The 60th attacked from Néhou towards St-Pierre-d'Arthéglise and Hills 145 and 133 which dominated the countryside, including the small town of Barneville-sur-Mer (now part of the combined Barneville-Carteret municipality). The efforts of Battle Group *Hellmich* to escape the impending American trap met with variable success, the US 39th Infantry Regiment engaging successfully with German units heading south just north of St-Jacques-de-Néhou. The actions and movements at this time of the three battalions of 60th Infantry Regiment are featured in greater detail in Tour A (*see pages 121–36*).

Progress was good and during the evening of 16 June (at 2210 hours according to one account) Maj Gen Collins instructed 9th Infantry Division to keep advancing. Maj Gen Eddy indicated that the advance was to continue with the words 'we're going all the way tonight'. 3rd Battalion, 60th Infantry Regiment, was instructed to push on to Barneville. At 2300 hours 47th Infantry Regiment moved south to St-Sauveur-le Vicomte with 3/47th Infantry pushing on and continuing its march south-west towards the village of St-Sauveur-de-Pierrepont, encountering sporadic resistance along the way. Nonetheless, 2/47th and 3/47th moved towards their main objective, the road junction north-east of St-Lô-d'Ourville.

Two German soldiers lie dead in their staff car in the St-Sauveur-le-Vicomte area. (USNA)

The memorial to men of the US 9th Infantry Division beside the D42 road to Barneville. This is a comparatively new monument, erected in 1998. *(Author)*

The cutting of the peninsula was achieved in remarkably quick time. 9th Infantry Division had performed extremely well. The retreating elements of the German 77th Infantry Division were heavily shelled by artillery of 60th Field Artillery Battalion and strafed by Allied fighter-bombers while German infantry units were engaged by US infantry at other points. These actions, involving the death of 77th Division's commanding officer, GenLt Rudolf Stegmann, largely prevented any escape by German units from the northern Cotentin. German indecision days earlier had left the retreat until too late and LXXXIV Corps paid a heavy price. The main exception to the American success in making the sealing the peninsula complete was the audacious escape by some 1,400 men, many of them from 1050th Grenadier Regiment. The new commander of 77th Division, *Oberst* (Colonel) Rudolf Bacherer, led this unit, accompanied by over 100 American prisoners of war. This escape was aided in part by the confusion surrounding the relief of 47th Infantry Regiment by 357th Infantry Regiment of 90th Infantry Division.

Lieutenant Colonel Michael B. Kauffman, commanding officer of 2nd Battalion, 60th Infantry Regiment, had this to say about why his men were able to perform in the fashion they did, while the units they replaced of 90th Infantry Division did not.

'How did the 9th succeed so quickly where the 90th had failed? Because they did not let mortar and small arms fire pin them down; because they took their casualties and kept pushing ahead; because they were willing to ignore snipers and small pockets of resistance and to push onto the main objectives, leaving these minor if annoying matters to be cleared up later.'

Source: Interview with Kauffman, 9th Infantry Division combat interviews; RG 407, Box 24026, Folder 53, US National Archives.

A US 155-mm gun pounding the defenders of Cherbourg from comparatively close range. While the US Army was well provided for in terms of artillery and had ample supplies of ammunition, this overwhelming superiority in terms of matériel did not necessarily equate to instant battlefield success. Well dug-in and adept at maximising the terrain advantages, the defenders still managed to inflict significant casualties on the Americans and delay Cherbourg's capture until the maximum damage had been done to its port facilities. *(USNA)*

This determination to push on regardless, with the principal objective being the overriding aim, served 9th Infantry Division well and in the Norman countryside it helped to deny the Germans the advantage that the terrain naturally presented.

CHAPTER 4

THE BATTLE FOR CHERBOURG

In its original form the American plan to seize Cherbourg envisaged the employment of just two infantry divisions with armour and artillery support, advancing to the east and west of the city – these being 4th Infantry Division to the left/west and

9th Infantry Division to the right/east. On 18 June, however, at a meeting between Generals Bradley and Collins and various divisional commanders, it was decided that the drive to take Cherbourg would instead incorporate three divisions in a line-abreast formation. First US Army Field Order No. 2 of 18 June set out the plan and allocated the units for the attack on Cherbourg. The advance north involved 4th Infantry Division on the right (the eastern side of the Cotentin), 79th Infantry Division in the centre and 9th Infantry Division on the left flank. The change in plan owed much to concerns about German troop dispositions plus the unready state of 90th Infantry Division and the freshness of 79th Infantry Division, which had landed in France on 14 June. On the right flank of 4th Infantry Division, American armour in the form of 24th Cavalry Squadron screened the advance, with 4th Cavalry Squadron (both squadrons were part of 4th Cavalry Group) committed to attack between 9th and 79th Infantry Divisions. This assault north involved a substantial force. In it, as the American official history makes clear, 'VII Corps would commit its full combat strength [to] the attack'.

German strength in Cherbourg and manning the surrounding defence perimeter was of patchy quality, much of it being made up of flak gun crews and naval personnel who no longer had any ships. The total figure for German forces was estimated to be between 25,000 and 40,000 men. While the Americans were unsure of the number of German defenders they were reasonably well informed as to their dispositions, possessing maps illustrating German strongpoints and defensive lines, derived from the extensive intelligence provided by French resistance groups and aerial photography pre-invasion and from recently captured German documents.

The plan to seize Cherbourg called for the main attack to begin at 0500 hours on 19 June with 9th Infantry Division's objective being the high ground between the towns of Rauville-la-Bigot and St-Germain-le-Gaillard. For 79th Infantry Division, objectives centred on the high ground west and north-west of Valognes and to advance to these objectives the division was to pass through 90th Infantry Division that was already *in situ*. On the right flank 4th Infantry Division was to advance north to Montebourg and was to begin the attack at 0300 hours without a preceding artillery barrage. The terrain south of Cherbourg, in the area to be covered by both 9th and 79th Infantry Divisions, is characterised by hills that dominate the roads, the main avenues of advance, and is particularly suited to defensive efforts. The German Seventh Army's war diary summarised events on 18 June by concluding that the inevitable American assault on Cherbourg would not come from the direction of Quinéville and Montebourg but from the south-west.

Wrecked buildings and vehicles in Montebourg, north-west of Utah Beach. The initial US plan to take Cherbourg envisaged a drive in this direction from Utah to Cherbourg, but determined German resistance in front of Montebourg eventually necessitated the lengthy diversion across the Cotentin peninsula. The damage inflicted on Montebourg was typical of the level of destruction across Normandy in 1944. It perhaps explains the, at times, lukewarm reception given by the locals to the Allied troops who had come to 'liberate' them from the Germans. *(USNA)*

The US 4th Infantry Division, meanwhile, was preparing to capitalise on what appeared to be a deteriorating German position and move its 8th and 12th Infantry Regiments to the west and east, respectively, of Montebourg, attacking early that morning. Both regimental attacks took place on schedule but at dawn the elements of 12th Infantry Regiment were held by strong German resistance along the east–west rail line, just to the north-west of the town. This line was manned by men from 729th Grenadier Regiment and from Seventh Army Assault Battalion, with an estimated strength of between 1,000 and 1,500 men. Eventually, after considerable difficulty in dealing with enemy

THE ADVANCE ON CHERBOURG, 21–25 JUNE
0
1
2
Kilometres
US POSITIONS
21 June, 2400 hours
22 June, 2400 hours
23 June, 2400 hours
24 June, 2400 hours
25 June, 2400 hours
German defensive perimeter (approx.)
Urville-Hague
Nacqueville
Querqueville
Pointe et Fort de Querqueville
Fort de l'Ouest
Equeurdreville
Henneville
Tonneville
Branville
Ste Croix-Hague
Flottemanville-Hague
Acqueville
Nouainville
Grimesnil
Sideville
Martinvast
Gourbesville
Gruchy
Aux Ducs
Landemer
Christo
Capel
Eudal
Es Petits
Leveille
Lucas
Mouchel
Bas Village
Rue d'Ozouville
les Tours
Traisnellerie
Herville
le Coudray
la Judée
les Contes
les Terriers
la Haye
Voisin
Neretz
Boguenville
Launay
Baudretot
Vaitot
Flague
Nee
la Belière
les Poitevins
Noires Vaches
Querqueville
la Rivière
Antreville
la Coquerie
le Hamelet
Haut Biville
la Cx Frimot
Moulin
le Val Fabien
Lieu Piquot
Rue de Gréville
Lieu Bailly
Fleury
Bosvy
Samson
la Quiesce
Cousin
Noel
Bois du Mt du Roc
Cape
la Lande
la Jouannerie
Hardinvast
la Motterie
Tollevast
1
2
3
6

1 60th Infantry Regiment, 9th Infantry Division
2 47th Infantry Regiment, 9th Infantry Division
3 39th Infantry Regiment, 9th Infantry Division
4 313th Infantry Regiment, 79th Infantry Division
5 314th Infantry Regiment, 79th Infantry Division
6 315th Infantry Regiment, 79th Infantry Division
7 8th Infantry Regiment, 4th Infantry Division
8 12th Infantry Regiment, 4th Infantry Division
9 22nd Infantry Regiment, 4th Infantry Division
Base maps: GSGS 4250 Beaumont-Hamel 5E2, Les Pieux 5E4, Cherbourg 6E1, Valognes 6E3&4
Cap Lévy
Fort de l'Ile Pelée
Digue
Fort des Flamands
Tourlaville
Digosville
Maupertus
Gonneville
Fermanville
Carneville
Bretteville
la Glace
Mesnil au Val
le Theil
Rufosses
la Bourdonnerie
Hau Auvray
Hau Puchot
les Chevres
les Martins
Hau de Haut
Hau au Sage
Hau au Comte

soldiers both well dug-in and determined to fight, the US forces overcame German resistance. Montebourg itself was seized from the Germans at 1800 hours and the town was deserted when American forces entered it. The remnants of 729th Grenadier Regiment and Seventh Army Assault Battalion retreated into Cherbourg, where they were destroyed in due course. Neither was reformed.

The American advance in the west made faster progress with 9th Infantry Division in particular making ground and encountering little opposition from the enemy. At the end of the day 9th Infantry Division was well established in positions several kilometres beyond its initial objectives. In the centre of the US advance progress was far slower with 79th Infantry Division 'jumping off' from a start line between the small villages of Golleville and Urville, meeting resistance in front of 315th Infantry Regiment and ending up unable to sever the Valognes–Cherbourg road before nightfall. 4th Cavalry Squadron, operating in the vicinity of the small town of Néhou, moved north-west towards Bricquebec and eventually pushed well past that town to a point as far north as les Flagues, a small collection of houses along the main route (now the D900) to Cherbourg. At the end of 19 June, American forces stood on a rough line as far north as Helleville in the west to St-Martin-le-Gréard immediately south of Cherbourg and only some 6–8 km from the southern outskirts of the city. The American line then ran south-east to the Bois de la Brique (west of Valognes) and from there to Huberville (east of Valognes). 315th Infantry Regiment of 79th Infantry Division had by-passed the significant town of Valognes, as it did not fall within the division's boundary. 4th Infantry Division, within whose remit the town did fall, stopped just to the south-east of the town.

The objectives for US VII Corps for 20 June envisaged 79th Infantry Division completing its seizure of objectives north-west of Valognes and, using the Valognes–Cherbourg road as its axis of advance, moving north to occupy the high ground to the south of Cherbourg. 4th Infantry Division on the right flank of the American advance was to move towards the high ground to the south-east and east of Cherbourg with the intention of progressing, eventually, towards Tourlaville on the city's eastern outskirts. Similarly, in the west, 9th Infantry Division was to seize the high ground between Octeville and Flottemanville-Hague.

US vehicles in Valognes, 24 June. What would now be termed 'collateral damage' was wholly inevitable in the fighting in the northern Cotentin and indeed across Normandy, given the nature of the terrain and the Allies' German enemy. *(USNA)*

As the American forces moved forward on 20 June it became increasingly apparent in the east now, as had been demonstrated in the west the previous day, that many of the German formations had largely disengaged and retreated northwards into the 'fortress' of Cherbourg itself. This was especially true of the town of Valognes, when eventually American patrols from 1st Battalion, 8th Infantry Regiment, entered the town on the morning of 20 June.

The three American divisions and their constituent infantry units gradually pushed ahead and endeavoured to take up positions on the high ground around Cherbourg. As they did so they encountered the perimeter of German defences on the land side of the port. These were frequently quite extensive arrangements and were integrated into the landscape, making much use of rivers and other natural barriers to thwart any easy progress. The Germans had also dug ditches and blocked roads and tracks with barriers. The German perimeter described an east–west arc running through the following towns and positions: Cap Lévi–Maupertus–Bois du Coudray–Hill 178–the upper Trottebec River– Hardinvast–Martinvast–Sideville–Hills 128 and 131–Flottemanville-Hague–Ste-Croix-Hague–Branville–Hameau Gruchy. While this sounds impressive, and indeed, plotted on a map, looks substantial, it must also be remembered that the forces available to GenLt von Schlieben were a rag-tag collection of elements of various units, many of which were either *Ost* battalions and/or static formations. It was difficult, therefore, for US planners to gauge likely levels of resistance as good defensive positions alone were not necessarily a sound guide.

American troops in the ruins of Valognes following its liberation. One man is holding up a bottle of champagne in what appears to be a rather half-hearted effort to celebrate. (*USNA*)

Accordingly, during the evening of 20 June, Maj Gen Collins sensibly instructed his forces to begin to probe the extent of German defences and in particular, to ascertain the quality and quantity of the German troops manning these defences, as it was these particular pieces of information that were most needed by American intelligence.

American forces thus began, on 21 June, with vigorous patrols into German-held territory, the German forces responding to American incursions with similar vim and vigour. The Americans also reorganised their units with 4th Cavalry Squadron moving from les Flagues (and being replaced by 3rd Battalion, 39th Infantry Regiment) to the area of l'Epinette at the western end of the German defensive perimeter. In the centre of the corps' front 315th Infantry Regiment had moved as far north as St-Martin-le-Gréard before encountering stiff resistance and then settling for penning German forces in their positions rather than progressing further.

In the eastern Cotentin 4th Infantry Division pushed ahead as far north as was possible, intent on determining the exact boundaries of the German defensive arrangements and what comprised the principal German line. On 21 June, 22nd Infantry Regiment moved north to cut Cherbourg off from the eastern portion of the northern Cotentin. This action is described in detail in Tour B (*see pages 136–50*).

The American forces had now effectively invested the fortress of Cherbourg, surrounding it on virtually all sides and facing its outer defensive perimeter. Such was the ferocity and intensity of the artillery fire on Cherbourg and approaches that all electricity and water supplies to the city proper failed, prompting the Germans to deploy emergency units to restore supplies. The scene was set for the final showdown, with the prize for the Allies the vital harbour facilities so important to the Allied war effort.

Sergeant R.D. Shelton examines a captured example of the feared German *Panzerschreck* anti-tank weapon. (*USNA*)

For the German defenders of Cherbourg, whether in the extensive line of blockhouses and forts or in the town itself, the situation was bleak. Hopes of relief from the south were unrealistic as all German efforts now focused upon ensuring that the Allied position in the Cotentin was unable to develop further. The Germans' own assessment in Seventh Army's war diary was that, 'Fortress Cherbourg has supplies for 56 days calculated on its present strength'. Seventh Army command estimated that, 'the enemy has 6½ divisions at his disposal for the attack on Cherbourg. The bulk of the enemy will be committed against von Schlieben.'

On the night of 21 June came the first act in the taking of Cherbourg. Maj Gen Collins sent a message to GenLt von Schlieben, the commander of the German ground forces. Collins candidly pointed out the position that von Schlieben was in – isolated from the rest of the German forces and surrounded by the Americans. Collins demanded that the German forces in and around Cherbourg surrender, with his ultimatum expiring at 0900 hours on 22 June. This message was also broadcast to the defenders and, in a reflection of the heterogeneous composition of the 'German' forces, was transmitted in Polish, French and Russian as well as German.

A view of the storm-twisted Loebnitz pier (floating roadway) of the Mulberry harbour at Omaha, badly damaged by the storm. *(USNA)*

Collins did not place too much faith in the likely effects of this message and planned a massive assault on the city. The plan used some of the tremendous air power available to the Allied forces in Normandy and aimed to strike at the heavily defended areas to the north and east of Flottemanville-Hague and Martinvast;

the fortified positions at les Chèvres and the strongpoints to the south-west and south of the city known as 'C', a strong anti-aircraft position; 'D', the formidable Fort du Roule; and 'F', a strongpoint to the south of Cherbourg.

While Collins planned his assault and his men rested briefly, in the English Channel nature was intervening in the forthcoming battle for Cherbourg. A tremendous storm in the Channel effectively wrecked the Mulberry harbour in the American landing zone and also greatly delayed the landing of stores for the duration of the storm itself. On Omaha Beach alone 90 small ferries were driven ashore and across all the British and American beaches 800 vessels of all descriptions were beached as a result of the high winds and mountainous seas. The unloading effort was not renewed until 23 June and then only by the employment of amphibious vehicles capable of picking their way through the tangled debris of much of the artificial port. As a result of the storm, the Mulberry harbour off Omaha was abandoned for good. This, of course, gave renewed significance to the final assault on Cherbourg.

> **Major General Collins made this point crystal clear in his pre-attack address.**
>
> 'This attack on Cherbourg is the major effort of the American Army and is especially vital now that unloading across the beaches has been interfered with by the weather. All divisional commanders surely appreciate the importance of this attack.'
>
> *Source:* VII Corps G3 journal, 21 June 1944, cited in Gordon Harrison, *Cross-Channel Attack*, p. 246.

By the morning of 22 June the weather had improved slightly. At 0940 hours Collins considered that the change in the weather was sufficient to begin the attack on Cherbourg. The time of the assault was set at 1400 hours that day with a massive air bombardment beginning at 1240 hours. This involved Royal Air Force (RAF) and United States Army Air Force (USAAF) aircraft of Second Tactical Air Force and Ninth Air Force respectively. While hundreds of aircraft participated, the impressive concentration of air power was not matched by co-ordination with ground troops. Despite the fact that American ground forces had wisely retreated as much as 1,000 metres in many places in order to avoid problems of casualties from friendly fire, between 1300 and 1330 hours three separate infantry regiments, 47th and 60th to the south-west of Cherbourg and 22nd to the east, all radioed in to their headquarters to report that they were under fire from the Allied aircraft and all suffered casualties. These local problems were caused in part by the shifting of smoke markers due to a strong north-easterly wind. There were also problems of co-ordinating aircraft coming in from England and, indeed, the final air plan itself had been made in England, with its form and constraints only being made known when the plan itself was flown to Normandy on 22 June.

A dead German soldier lies in a Cherbourg street. The walls behind his body are pockmarked with bullet holes. The German's rifle lies beside his body and in his right hand he still holds a grenade. *(USNA)*

The main impact on the German defenders was disappointing in terms of physical damage; however, the attacks did succeed in cutting some German communications and certainly had a profound impact on morale. The American planners, who saw the defenders of Cherbourg as a polyglot force, fully aware of its desperate position, highlighted this consideration. Fundamentally, however, it was left to the men on the ground to achieve the act of reducing the city.

For 4th Infantry Division, advancing towards Cherbourg from the east, the primary objective was the Tourlaville area and this was the job given to 12th Infantry Regiment. Some 3.5 km to the south of Tourlaville 8th Infantry Regiment was to seize the high ground in the vicinity of la Glacerie, with the division's other infantry regiment, the 22nd, employed in support of the rear and right flank of the 12th.

This plan did not go smoothly. 12th Infantry Regiment made little progress against German defenders in the area of the Bois du Coudray, advancing only a few hundred metres at the very start of the US offensive. Lieutenant Colonel (Lt Col) Thaddeus R. Dulin, commanding 3rd Battalion, 12th Infantry Regiment, was killed by a German sniper while leading his men in a bayonet charge up a steep incline in an attempt to secure the defensive benefits of higher ground. Only after this loss was some form of order imposed by the surviving American commanders. Even then, the battalion was isolated from the rest of the regiment and only heavily escorted patrols, with tanks, were able to replenish it. Command of the battalion devolved onto the executive officer, Major Kenneth R. Lindner at this point.

Lieutenant Hay, from 3rd Battalion, 12th Infantry, detailed how his unit used tanks in support of its advance.

'Scout ahead to search the hedge rows for sticky-bombardiers and AT [anti-tank] riflemen; scouts motion tanks ahead, tanks proceed – spray next hedgerow generously and so on. When necessary, tanks sit quietly and remove obstacles with their 75s [75-mm main guns].'

Source: 4th Infantry Division combat interviews; RG 407-427, Box 24014, Folder 29, US National Archives.

The employment of tanks was also found to be similarly useful to 12th Infantry Regiment, having immediate benefits on 23 June as the German defenders were unable to counter them and were forced to flee. Seventh Army's war diary commented on this advance that the Americans 'received continuous reinforcements', in stark contrast to the resource-starved Germans, and that the Americans were 'supported by numerous tanks'.

In the centre of VII Corps' advance, 79th Infantry Division moved north between the Rivers Trottebec and Divette, with the aim of capturing Fort du Roule and the high ground to the south of the city. The route of 79th Infantry Division's main axis of advance was along the Valognes–Cherbourg main road. The

A Sherman tank advancing through the devastated streets of Cherbourg with the crew seemingly on the look-out for isolated snipers. A US Army Signal Corps photographer took this picture on 26 June, the day that GenLt von Schlieben surrendered himself and his headquarters – although not the garrison at large – to the Americans. The angle of this photo suggests that for all the posturing with the tank there is little danger from snipers (as the photographer would have had to be in an exposed position to secure the shot). *(USNA)*

latter portion of the advance, into the outskirts of the town, is discussed in Tour C (*see pages 150–67*).

There were three prepared defensive posts along this route that would have to be tackled by the Americans. The first was at les Chèvres, the second, about 2 km to the north, was at la Mare à Canards, and 2.5 km further north was the substantial Fort du Roule. This heavily defended location dominated the harbour and was lavishly provided for in terms of air defence. Additional areas of resistance could be found on both sides of the main road. The initial plan was for the division's three infantry regiments to advance in line abreast, the 315th on the left and the 313th on the right with the main effort concentrated on the 314th in the centre.

Throughout the day 314th Infantry Regiment made slow but steady progress before becoming halted at Tollevast. Attempts to go through resistance here proved futile and eventually the 1st and 3rd Battalions of 314th Infantry Regiment went around the German positions and settled on an east–west defensive position west of what was known as Crossroads 177, on modern roads the junction where the east–west D122 crosses the N13. In skirting the German positions these battalions of 314th Infantry found themselves cut off but soon re-established links with the main American force early on the morning of 23 June. The Germans, desperate to counter the advance, also moved up naval personnel (part of the garrison of the fortress) under cover of darkness in a bid to stem the American thrust.

Two US infantrymen, both armed with the M1 Garand semi-automatic rifle, move cautiously forward. The soldiers are wearing heavy coats because of the unseasonable cold weather, garments that did not aid ease of movement. (*USNA*)

The next major obstacle was the German strongpoint near la Mare à Canards, known as Position F. Allied dive-bombing attacks at 0900 hours had little effect and another attack, at 1100 hours, was hastily diverted north of the intended target after concerns had been expressed about the proximity of the forward American forces to the target. Nevertheless, A Company, 1/314th Infantry, managed to push on past the objective and occupy a ridge approximately 1–1.5 km to the north-west. Position F itself fell to the Americans the following day.

9th Infantry Division's objectives focused on Octeville and the high ground to the south-west of Cherbourg. By the night of 23 June the division had overcome fierce resistance around

Beaudienville. The 2nd and 3rd Battalions of 47th Infantry Regiment had made good progress to sit in defensive positions to the north-northwest of the Bois du Mont du Roc and in front of the small town of Nouainville. The capture of Hill 171 netted the regiment some 400 German POWs in the process. Here, according to German records, the 'last available reserves' of the Cherbourg garrison were deployed to halt the attack. 1st and 2nd Battalions of 60th Infantry Regiment had also progressed to halt in an arc to the north-west of Flottemanville-Hague.

However, the act of by-passing strongpoints of enemy resistance caused some problems for the Americans, who had to clear German positions that threatened lines of communication behind their axes of advance. According to the Seventh Army war diary German soldiers caught behind the American advance were instructed 'to continue the fight in the rear of the enemy and to maintain pockets of resistance'.

THE FALL OF CHERBOURG

On 23 June GenLt von Schlieben relieved GenMaj Sattler (who then became von Schlieben's deputy) to take command of all German fighting forces in the Cherbourg 'fortress'.

> **As well as this enlarged command, von Schlieben also received a direct order from Supreme Commander Adolf Hitler.**
>
> 'Even if worst comes to worst it is your duty to defend the last bunker and leave to the enemy not a harbour but a field of ruins... the German people and the whole world are watching your fight; on it depends the conduct and result of operations to smash the beachheads and the honour of the German Army and of your own name.'
>
> *Source:* Seventh Army war diary, entry for 23 June 1944; RG 407, Box 24154, Folder 488, US National Archives.

Despite these words of dubious encouragement, von Schlieben's position was dire. He requested additional men, supplies and air coverage but had little hope of receiving any. Von Schlieben outlined the inadequacies of his troops to Rommel and noted that many of the men under his command suffered from 'bunker paralysis', supposedly being unwilling or unable to operate effectively other than from their fixed defences. Brief

An M1 8-inch howitzer lets fly at German defences. This weapon had a range of almost 17 km and fired a shell weighing some 90 kg (200 lb). *(USNA)*

consideration was given to moving the 15th Paratroop (*Fallschirmjäger*) Regiment by sea from St-Malo to Cherbourg but this was always unrealistic in the face of total Allied command of the sea and of the air. A plan to drop them from the air was rejected for similar reasons. Even the fact of von Schlieben's promotion to fortress commander caused problems for the Germans. Although von Schlieben informed Sattler in person that he had taken over, it took several days for the scattered German forces in and around Cherbourg to be informed that all decisions and command reports should now be directed to von Schlieben and not Sattler. Contemporary German documents indicated that, 'the troops were not sufficiently informed of the change in commanding officer and much valuable time was lost by messages and reports being misdirected to GenMaj Sattler.'

No sooner had von Schlieben arrived to take command than the headquarters switchboard became alive with messages from German positions on the outskirts of the Cherbourg defensive line reporting heavy American air and artillery attacks. Several

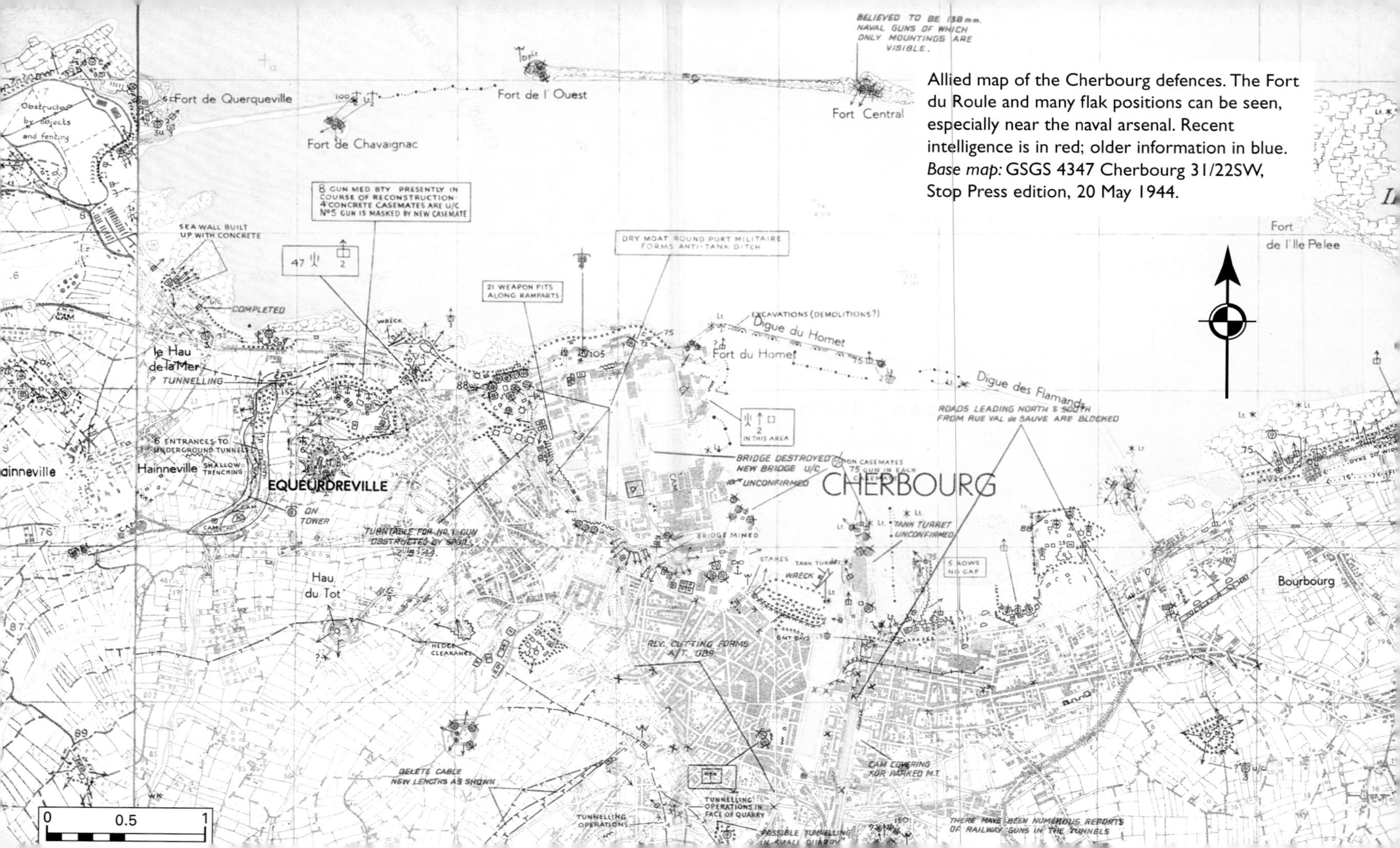

Allied map of the Cherbourg defences. The Fort du Roule and many flak positions can be seen, especially near the naval arsenal. Recent intelligence is in red; older information in blue. *Base map:* GSGS 4347 Cherbourg 31/22SW, Stop Press edition, 20 May 1944.

German bunkers contacted von Schlieben to inform him that not only were they surrounded by US troops, and cut off from other German positions, but also that the Americans had barricaded the doors to the strongpoints, preventing the defenders inside from escaping. German units, in what the Germans themselves termed this 'embarrassing situation', were given permission by GenLt von Schlieben to hoist the white flag and surrender.

The German forces surrounded in Cherbourg and environs numbered approximately 21,000 men at this point, according to the Seventh Army's war diary of 22 June. This figure was 'composed of the fort garrison and remnants of 709th Infantry Division, as well as parts of 91st Airlanding, 77th and 243rd Infantry Divisions'. It should be noted that 21,000 men is considerably lower than the upper limits of the US estimates.

Additional German measures in Cherbourg included the evacuation of large numbers of French civilians, leaving only around 6,000 (from a population of 40,000) inside the encirclement and leaving clear 'free-fire' zones. Prior to the final withdrawal into the defensive perimeter the Germans had also tried to secure more cattle, in preparation for what they may have believed would be a long siege. Ammunition supplies were still dangerously low, with little additional ammunition having been brought to Cherbourg, in particular by von Schlieben's own battle group at the time of its withdrawal into the defensive perimeter. The most urgent requirement for the beleaguered Germans, according to the Seventh Army war diary, was 'anti-tank weapons and 80-mm mortar ammunition'. None, however, was to be forthcoming. Cherbourg and its surrounded garrison were on their own.

By the morning of 24 June, VII Corps was in a position to push on to the outskirts of the city of Cherbourg itself, having more or less either cleared or by-passed all effective German resistance in the shrinking defensive arc that ringed the city on its landward side. The American official history states that, at this point, 'the whole Cherbourg defence was collapsing and nowhere more completely than in the east'. This was true in the grand scheme of things but that gradual collapse was a result of relentless American pressure and hard fighting.

On the right flank 12th Infantry Regiment moved north-west towards Tourlaville, encountering several German positions between there and Digosville. K Company of 3rd Battalion, 12th

Infantry Regiment, supported by four tanks, came under heavy fire east of Digosville before suppressing the defence with the aid of 12 P-47 Thunderbolts. By the evening of 24 June 12th Infantry Regiment overlooked the whole city of Cherbourg from the east and on instructions from Maj Gen Raymond O. Barton, commanding 4th Infantry Division, this regiment moved, unopposed, into the town of Tourlaville. During the course of the fighting on 24 June the 12th had captured more than 800 German prisoners.

8th Infantry Regiment encountered stiff resistance east of la Glacerie and lost 37 killed on 24 June including a battalion commander, Lt Col Conrad Simmons of 1st Battalion. Meanwhile 3rd Battalion, 8th Infantry, had an interesting experience of German tactics during its early morning attack. The battalion had been promised tank support but, as this failed to arrive by the appointed H-Hour of 0700 hours, the infantry went in unsupported. L Company found many German soldiers ‘pretending to be dead’ as they progressed ‘lying heel to heel, with mgs [machine guns] and other arms’. The battalion executive officer, Major Fred Collins, later the battalion commander, explained that these Germans were ‘discovered’ only after the main battalion force had moved through the area and the men of L Company were alarmed to find seven ‘dead’ Germans suddenly standing up and surrendering. Collins believed that the intention was to allow the Americans to advance and then to strike at their rear. The discovery of this German ruse undoubtedly saved many American lives and probably the impetus of this particular advance.

In the centre 313th Infantry Regiment was busily engaging a whole succession of German strongpoints located to the west of la Glacerie and at Hameau Gringore slightly to the north, taking 320 prisoners on the way as well as capturing some German artillery. Attempts by 314th Infantry Regiment to strike out towards Fort du Roule, after capturing Strongpoint F at la Mare à Canards, were hampered by heavy German fire directed from the Octeville area across the river, although close air support from USAAF Thunderbolts aided the American cause. To the south-west the Germans still held out at Hardinvast, only succumbing on 25 June, and 315th Infantry Regiment was delayed considerably there in relation to the division’s other infantry units.

US infantry look on at a dead German soldier, killed during the bitter fighting on the southerly approaches to the Fort du Roule. *(USNA)*

An American war correspondent attached to 79th Infantry Division filed this report as he accompanied the advance into the burning city.

'Rain was falling on our faces when we awakened. It was a cold, gray misty dawn. The column was forming up in the mud for the final advance into Cherbourg. We moved forward into a deserted quarter of the city, evidently a section in which working people had lived. Concussion had shattered every window, every bit of glass. The telephone and electric light wires were broken tangles. But most of the buildings did not appear to have been damaged seriously by either the bombings or the shellfire. The Germans had bricked up many windows and doors, leaving only narrow embrasures from which machine-guns would sweep the street.'

Grimy US infantrymen dug in on the upper levels of the Fort du Roule on 26 June, shortly after its surrender. *(USNA)*

The narrow and frequently steep streets of Cherbourg, held by a determined and skilled opponent, were likely to cause many problems for the Americans and likely to make the ground taken to date look to have been won comparatively easily.

Meanwhile, over on the left flank of the American advance, 9th Infantry Division was also edging slowly towards the outskirts of Cherbourg. Despite continued dogged German resistance 39th and 47th Infantry Regiments had managed to advance along the spur of high ground to the north-west of Octeville, overrunning three *Luftwaffe* flak units in the process, though these put up some moderate resistance. Meanwhile 60th Infantry Regiment held and cleared the north-western flank of the American attack, hanging back and digging in on high ground to the north of the small village of Flottemanville-Hague.

Overnight 39th and 47th Infantry Regiments, moving ahead and to the east of 60th Infantry Regiment, slowly penetrated the south-western suburbs of the city. The 39th dug in outside of Octeville while the 47th prepared to assault the fortified area known as the Redoute des Fourches. Although 9th Infantry Division had made good progress, VII Corps' orders held that the division should not attempt to enter the city before first light the next day.

Although German resistance was crumbling it was doing so only slowly and, given the urban environment, even comparatively few defenders could hinder much larger numbers of attackers for quite prolonged periods. The Americans, where possible, used overwhelming firepower to silence German defenders rather than risking men unnecessarily assaulting houses. Seventh Army's war diary managed to identify several major concerns in its ability to maintain resistance in Cherbourg: 'The numerous losses of unit leaders, heaviest artillery fire and ceaseless air attacks have lately been causing a general reduction in our capacity to resist.' As well as these American-inflicted problems the Germans also found that the will to fight was evaporating among certain of their units with, unsurprisingly, the 'eastern units... no longer capable of resisting'.

Seventh Army's assessment of the situation in Cherbourg was bleak but realistic. On 24 June Seventh Army's war diary claimed that, 'it cannot be doubted any longer that the enemy will force a breakthrough into the heart of the city on June 25.' With this acknowledgement of the inevitability of the eventual defeat, GenLt von Schlieben's continued demands for reinforcements were cancelled. This despite the fact that there had been little realistic hope of these demands being fulfilled, such was the strength of the Allied air and naval presence – the only two conceivable avenues of reinforcement. Henceforth, the explicit aim of continued resistance in the fortress of Cherbourg was that the battle should be sustained as long as possible so as to ensure that the maximum amount of damage could be done to the port's facilities, thus denying them to the Allies. German forces were also instructed to resist 'until the last round' and kill as many American attackers as possible. The decision to abandon the attempt to hold the port and reconstitute the fighting in terms of an attritional battle was simply a reflection of the realities of the situation for the Germans. They knew that, once the city of

Cherbourg had fallen, then the Americans would turn south. Every American casualty at Cherbourg meant one American soldier less to fight in the future. The daily summary of events by Seventh Army reported that, 'General von Schlieben has given the order that every pocket of resistance is to be defended to the last man. This must be done even if the pockets of resistance are practically surrounded by enemy units.'

On 25 June, in the centre of VII Corps' position, the main event of the day was the successful operation to seize the Fort du Roule. The action to secure the upper levels of this imposing fortress is discussed in greater detail in Tour C (*see pages 160–6*).

As a result of the collective action of 2nd Battalion, 314th Infantry, in the taking of Fort du Roule Collins recommended the battalion for a Unit Citation, which was duly bestowed by President Roosevelt. The final line asserts that, 'The Second Battalion's speedy and effective reduction of this strongpoint aptly described by the enemy as impregnable, was a magnificent display of courage and devotion to duty.'

German fortifications south of the Fort du Roule, photographed on 28 June. Supported by P-47 Thunderbolts, 3/314th attacked this position at 0800 hours on 25 June. During the assault, 1st Lieutenant Carlos O. Ogden of K/314th won the Medal of Honor. Twice wounded, he destroyed an 88-mm gun and several machine-gun nests with rifle fire and hand grenades. *(USNA)*

On the left of 2nd Battalion the 3rd moved up in support and a Medal of Honor was won, this time by 1st Lieutenant Carlos C. Ogden. Ogden had only just assumed command of his company and, among other exploits, managed to manoeuvre into a position to fire a rifle grenade into a particularly troublesome bunker, destroying an 88-mm gun.

The top level of the Fort du Roule surrendered eventually with last resistance being extinguished around 2200 hours on the evening of 25 June. Meanwhile 313th Infantry Regiment moved from Hameau Gringore and into the south-east of Cherbourg but the guns of the lower levels of the Fort du Roule hindered further progress.

On the left flank 9th Infantry Division had mixed results on 25 June. 39th Infantry Regiment made some limited gains but soon become halted on the northern outskirts of Octeville. 47th Infantry Regiment, after advancing with the 39th, made a turn to the north and, by contrast, made comparatively rapid progress and seized German positions at Equeurdreville after limited fighting at Hameau du Tot.

> **The fortress at Equeurdreville certainly looked impressive. Interviews with officers from the 2nd Battalion, 47th Infantry Regiment, painted this picture.**
>
> '... 500 yards ahead loomed the Equeurdreville fort like a medieval fortification, on high ground overlooking the whole port area, the Arsenal etc with a dry moat surrounding it, barbed wire, one bridge and gate to the fort itself, overhanging observation rooms, tunnels reaching to the coastal batteries just to the north which it controlled.'
>
> *Source:* 9th Infantry Division, Normandy Action; RG 407, Box 24026, Folder 53, US National Archives.

The attack to secure the fort involved only one company, E Company of 2/47th Infantry. The company's three platoons attacked with 3rd Platoon on the left and the 2nd on the right with 1st Platoon directly behind. These latter two units were to assault the fortress' only entrance at the gate on the far side of the bridge over the dry moat. Aircraft pounded the fort in advance of the attack and mortars also shelled the fort in a creeping barrage. Storming through the gate, the Americans encountered some resistance, frequently from determined individuals rather than co-ordinated forces, and by 1130 hours had taken 70-odd prisoners and secured the position. In their area of operations as a whole, 9th Infantry Division's formations took more than 1,100 prisoners.

The struggle to secure the bitterly contested Fort des Flamands demonstrated how much of a battle even a handful of relatively under-equipped soldiers could put up if they made the most of their defensive positions and possessed a will to fight. This photograph of the fort was taken on 30 June and the impact of ceaseless US air and artillery bombardment is only too apparent. *(USNA)*

So successful had been 4th Infantry Division's progress towards Cherbourg from the south-east and east that, on the afternoon of 25 June, Collins re-drew the divisional boundaries between 79th Infantry and 4th Infantry Divisions in order to allow the 4th to join the attack into Cherbourg. On the evening of 25 June, all three battalions of 12th Infantry Regiment moved into the eastern outskirts of Cherbourg and penetrated as far as the Rue de la Bretonnière, the pre-determined extent of any 4th Infantry Division advances into the town itself. At the Fort des Flamands, at the eastern end of the inner breakwater, resistance continued overnight with the defenders destroying facilities in the area. Only at 0550 hours on the 26th did the Germans begin to surrender and then only after witnessing US tanks demolishing beach bunkers at point-blank range. Some 350 German defenders came out of their positions with their hands in the air as a result. The Germans described the fighting in this area as 'furious'.

The Fort des Flamands, photographed from the air on 29 June. *(USNA)*

On the morning of 26 June the American forces in and around Cherbourg steeled themselves for what was to prove the final act in the battle. 79th Infantry Division arrayed to the east of the River Divette entered the city early and, by 0800 hours, 313th Infantry Regiment had reached as far as the eastern harbour area with the 314th also reaching the seafront by mid-afternoon.

American progress through the city was still hampered by the guns of the lower levels of Fort du Roule and 2/314th Infantry resumed its efforts to subdue entirely the forbidding fortress. This activity largely eschewed conventional fighting and became a process of introducing explosives into the fortress in such a fashion as to do the most damage. To this end explosives were lowered down ventilation shafts and suspended in front of gun openings and then detonated. A combination of these actions, plus the work of dedicated demolition teams and artillery fire, led to the final surrender of the fort in the early part of the evening with several hundred German defenders going into captivity.

In the east 22nd Infantry Regiment attacked the airport at Maupertus-sur-Mer and scored several impressive triumphs. One of the most notable achievements was that of 2nd Battalion, 22nd Infantry Regiment, which successfully secured the extensive system of bunkers known as the *Osteck*, on the high ground to the north of the airfield. The fighting here is discussed in greater detail in Tour B (*see pages 143–50*).

German soldiers emerging from underground positions, this time on 27 June (according to the official caption). This picture shows positions at the base of the Montagne du Roule immediately below the fortress itself. The open doorways in the background, beyond the heap of rubble and the surrendering German soldier, lead directly into the complex. (*USNA*)

Also on 26 June another major development occurred – the surrender of the German commander, GenLt von Schlieben, himself. His surrender was secured by 39th Infantry Regiment, whose main objectives were sandwiched between the River Divette and the area of activity of 47th Infantry Regiment further west. Information came to the Americans from German prisoners, quite by chance, of von Schlieben's whereabouts. The general was, in fact, ensconced in a bunker in the St-Sauveur area of the southern outskirts of Cherbourg city. The bunker was reached in mid-afternoon and a German prisoner was sent to attempt to persuade von Schlieben to surrender. Von Schlieben's initial response was to refuse to surrender and the Americans, in turn, replied with tank destroyers firing directly into the tunnel entrances of von Schlieben's shelter. This, together with obvious American preparations to demolish the structure with explosives, prompted the Germans sheltering inside finally to give up and

GenLt von Schlieben (in front) and *Konteradmiral* Hennecke are led away to captivity after their surrender. Both men show the dirt and strain of the weeks of fighting but both have put on their best uniforms, with von Schlieben's Knight's Cross prominently displayed. *(USNA)*

among the 850 who stumbled out was von Schlieben himself, accompanied by the senior German naval commander for Normandy, *Konteradmiral* (Rear Admiral) Walther Hennecke. The probable location of GenLt von Schlieben's bunker is identified in the Battlefield Tours section (*see page 117*).

The captive von Schlieben was taken at once to 9th Division's command post and immediately encouraged by Maj Gen Eddy to surrender the whole of Cherbourg. He demurred, claiming that communications with his forces were so poor that it would be impossible to contact his widely scattered men. Earnest American assurances that they could provide adequate communications to overcome these potential problems were still met with a resolute refusal by von Schlieben.

Seventh Army's war diary recorded the loss of the fortress commander.

'We received the last message from Group von Schlieben: "Records and coding machine destroyed. Since then all connection with Cherbourg has ceased." According to German sources, von Schlieben had been obliged to participate in the actual battle for his command post and... personally fought with the troops with a weapon in his hand and refused twice to answer the American general's request to surrender.'

Source: German Seventh Army war diary; RG 407, Box 24154, ML 88, US National Archives.

GenLt von Schlieben was taken to Collins' command post and asked a similar question, again refusing to surrender. Apparently von Schlieben claimed that his experiences in Russia led him to believe that his men could still continue to fight on and offer meaningful resistance. Von Schlieben's next port of call was Lt Gen Omar Bradley's HQ where Bradley famously refused to entertain von Schlieben to dinner, claiming, 'If the bastard had surrendered four days ago I'd have asked him [to dinner]. Now that he has cost us a pile of human lives – hell no!'

The surrender of von Schlieben and his bunker troops, as well as that of the city hall, which had been fortified and quite well manned by the Germans, left only the formidable arsenal complex as a major source of German resistance in Cherbourg. The arsenal, actually the naval arsenal adjacent to the main port area, was located in the north-west of the city and was well protected by thick walls and ample weapons. The Americans planned to assault the arsenal with all three battalions of 47th Infantry Regiment early on the morning of 27 June. Given the overall situation for German forces in Cherbourg it was thought that likely levels of resistance might not be high, but the soldiers of 1/47th Infantry still prepared many pole and satchel charges in anticipation of stiff German opposition.

To test German resolve to continue fighting Colonel Smythe, commanding officer of the 47th Infantry, initially deployed only a single company, which received fire in return. The decision was made to attack in earnest but the efforts of a psychological warfare unit (which made good use of a loudspeaker system fitted to the back of a truck), and the appearance of an American tank, had the desired effect before the attack went in. The defenders were informed that their erstwhile commander, GenLt von Schlieben, had himself been captured and that further resistance was futile. They surrendered at 1000 hours with in the region of 400 men being taken prisoner. Interviews conducted with men from 1/47th's B Company, however, suggest that as many as 800 German POWs may have been taken at the arsenal.

Requests made to the senior German officer there, GenMaj Sattler, to instruct other areas of resistance to cease fire were met with a refusal and Sattler also initially refused to surrender to Colonel Smythe, instead demanding to see Maj Gen Eddy. Sattler claimed, as had von Schlieben, that he had no means to order other parts of the fortress to surrender. While this claim, on the part of Sattler, was probably made for similar reasons to that of von Schlieben there would appear to be more circumstantial evidence to support Sattler's claim. Shortly after he had been

Then and now: An American soldier, identified as Private James Ferguson of Kentucky, shakes hands with a prisoner on 28 June while other Germans, apparently equally jovial, look on. The backdrop for this photo is the main entrance to the naval arsenal, the last major German position to surrender, and can be compared with the modern photograph above. *(USNA)*

relieved as fortress commander, Sattler moved his headquarters out of the cramped bunker in St-Sauveur/Octeville that he had been sharing with von Schlieben and re-established his command post in the arsenal. German sources suggest that, 'from this time on [24 June] until 27 June, when they were captured General Sattler and his staff obtained only very meagre bits of information about the progress of the action.'

In fact some of the forts in the inner and outer harbour continued to resist, in name at least. The harbour commander, a naval officer *Fregattenkapitän* (Commander, Senior Grade) Hans Witt, did not surrender, instead he ordered the wall along the docks to be sealed off and together with eight officers and 30 men crossed to the Fort de l'Ouest in a yacht and two small rowing boats. Once in Fort de l'Ouest he contacted his superiors at Naval Group West and informed them that he was ready to detonate the extensive minefields blocking the entrance to the western harbour. Witt's 'heroic' story was broadcast on German radio – and intercepted by the Americans who shelled the fort. Eventually, after three days, the fire control mechanism for the mines was destroyed and Witt surrendered.

The Fort de l'Ouest in Cherbourg harbour. It was to this impressive fortification that *Fregattenkapitän* Witt made his daring last-ditch escape as American forces closed in on Cherbourg's harbour area. The fort appears comparatively unscathed in this picture although piles of debris are apparent. (*USNA*)

The port city of Cherbourg was secured by the US Army's VII Corps at the cost of 22,119 casualties. Of these 2,811 were killed, 5,665 were listed as missing and 13,564 wounded. Some 39,042 Germans had been taken prisoner in Normandy by 1 July of whom 29,182 were taken by VII Corps. The Germans also had an undetermined number killed in the fighting for the town and since the landing on Utah Beach some 21 days previously. Following the successful capture of the city the American forces

28 June, and fires still rage in Cherbourg even after the German surrender. This picture, taken from the high ground to the east, shows the Atlantic terminal through the smoke of numerous fires in the centre of the port area. *(USNA)*

were faced with the daunting prospect of attempting to clean up the damage done by the German defenders in their efforts to deny the facilities of the port to the Allied war effort. In fact, the German Seventh Army Command had been arguing for the complete destruction of the port area of Cherbourg as early as 9 June, a mere three days after the Allied landings.

The American military engineer who wrote the plan for the repair and rehabilitation of the port noted: 'The demolition of the port of Cherbourg is a masterful job, beyond a doubt the most complete, intensive and best planned demolition in history.' This did not bode well for the Allied forces in Normandy. Adolf Hitler awarded the architect of this destruction, *Konteradmiral* Hennecke, the Knight's Cross for his actions, although at the time of the award Hennecke had been a prisoner of the Americans for 24 hours. Some indication of the amount of damage wrought by the Germans can be seen by the fact that every single basin, military or civilian, had at least one ship sunk in it and the largest had something in the region of 20,000 cubic metres of masonry and other material deposited into it as well as two large merchantmen sunk to block the entrance.

Total Battle Casualties VII Corps
6 June – 1 July 1944

Unit	Killed	Wounded	Missing	Captured	Total
4th Infantry Div	844	3,814	788	6	5,452
9th Infantry Div	301	2,061	76	–	2,438
79th Infantry Div	240	1,896	240	–	2,376
90th Infantry Div	386	1,979	34	–	2,399
82nd Airborne Div	457	1,440	2,571	12	4,480
101st Airborne Div	546	2,217	1,907	–	4,670
Corps personnel	37	157	49	61	304
Totals	2,811	13,564	5,665	79	22,119

Overlord plans had a requirement for the captured port to have received in the region of 150,000 tons of cargo by 25 July, yet it had only discharged 18,000 by that date. However, while the reconstruction efforts were initially slow as a result of the tremendous amount of damage done by the Germans, by November 1944 the port had landed 433,201 tons of supplies, more than half the total of all stores landed for the American forces in Europe. This amount averaged out at 14,500 tons a day, some 6,000 more than the 8,500 tons a day that had been estimated in the pre-invasion planning figures. Another useful comparative statistic that puts the reconstruction effort into perspective is that in 1937 the total amount of goods landed at Cherbourg was 325,000 tons.

The successful capture of the city of Cherbourg was described in 313th Infantry Regiment's official history.

'The stunned and shattered city of Cherbourg was quiet at last. The dust had settled and the last bullet had flown its deadly flight. The tenuous fingers of American might had at last reached the city's quivering throat and the last Nazi pulse was stilled at last!'

Source: 313th Infantry Regiment, Regimental History; RG 407, Box 24053, Folder 153, US National Archives.

On 27 June, before all German resistance had been totally extinguished, Maj Gen Collins organised a liberation ceremony in the Place Napoleon outside the city hall. Collins assembled all his divisional commanders and presented the mayor of Cherbourg, Paul Reynaud, with a French tricolour made up of parachute

silks from the various US airborne units that had landed in France. In his autobiography Collins noted that, after the ceremonies, one of his divisional commanders, Maj Gen 'Billy' Wyche, said: 'Joe, I didn't know you could speak French. I could understand every word you said.' Collins in self-deprecating fashion simply replied, 'That's bad news, Billy, because if the Americans could understand me the Frenchmen could not.'

Cherbourg citizens eagerly assist US soldiers in pulling down the sign advertising the headquarters of the Todt labour organisation in Cherbourg, 27 June. *(USNA)*

CHAPTER 5

FIGHTING AFTER THE FALL OF CHERBOURG

Operations in the North

While the surrender of the port city of Cherbourg achieved one of the main aims of Operation Neptune, pockets of German resistance still remained to the east and west of the city itself. The main effort of VII Corps was focused, obviously, upon the town itself but in the west the German forces in the Cap de la Hague area were successfully bottled up through the efforts of 4th Cavalry Group and 60th Infantry Regiment which had pushed on to the coast to the west of Cherbourg and succeeded in isolating the peninsula from the rest of the fighting. In the east a similar screening exercise was also conducted by 22nd Infantry Regiment and 24th Cavalry Squadron.

The 22nd Infantry Regiment fought in some of the heaviest engagements in these 'peripheral' actions of which the seizure of the German held airfield at Maupertus-sur-Mer proved to be one of the hardest. The 22nd attacked on 25 June and only finally overcame enemy resistance on 27 June. The substantial 'Hamburg' battery, some 2 km south of Cap Lévi, was shelled into submission by American artillery and surrendered, with 900 German sailors taken prisoner. Organised German resistance to the east of Cherbourg ceased with the surrender of the 'Hamburg' complex and speculative American patrols as far east as the small fishing port of Barfleur on the coast found this area was unoccupied by German troops.

The view, looking north from the 'York' battery near Amfréville, just west of Cherbourg, one of the first American objectives during the clearance of Cap de la Hague. Events in this area are more fully discussed in Tour D. (*Author*)

The American official history comments that, 'The clearing of Cap de la Hague was expected to be more difficult for it was estimated that about 3,000 enemy troops still held out there.' As it transpired, however, German troop totals in the Cap de la Hague peninsula were more than double this figure and in fact serious preparations were undertaken by the Germans to continue resistance here for as long as was possible, even though Cherbourg had fallen and the efforts of German forces in this area could no longer exercise any useful impact on the course of the campaign in the northern Cotentin. Even as the fighting in Cherbourg ceased as German units either surrendered or were wiped out, plans were being made to continue the fight in what the Germans termed the 'Jobourg peninsula'. (This area was sometimes called the 'electronic' peninsula by Germans and local French citizens alike, so packed was it with electronic eavesdropping equipment monitoring Allied transmissions across the Channel.)

The commanding officer of German forces in the peninsula, *Oberstleutnant* (Lt Col) Günther Keil, had plans as late as 24–25 June to 'reorganise the available forces during the night of 25/26 June, in order to make it possible to continue the defence of the Jobourg peninsula'. 9th Infantry Division was given the job of clearing the peninsula and launched operations on 29 June with resistance being comparatively light until American troops reached the outskirts of Beaumont-Hague. Outflanking operations and brave infantry action against well dug-in defenders, able to deploy considerable defensive fire, eventually saw 60th Infantry Regiment prevail. The strongest of several well-considered German positions in this area was the fortified locality in the region of the small villages of Gréville and Hameau Gruchy. The connected strongpoints and bunkers here were sometimes referred to as the *Westeck*. While this title confirmed the fact that these villages provided the western anchor of the Cherbourg defensive perimeter, the *Westeck* was very much the poor relation of its cousin to the east, the *Osteck*. Today little remains of the *Westeck* fortifications while the *Osteck* still dominates the area north of the Cherbourg airport at Maupertus.

Continuing American attacks across the peninsula by 60th and 47th Infantry Regiments and 4th Cavalry Group inevitably ground down the defenders, many of whom, according to contemporary German sources, 'were little used to team work and have almost no combat experience... [they] cannot hold up for long against an enemy who has material superiority.' While the persistent German references to the overwhelming abundance of American matériel are perfectly accurate this does not tell the whole story. The American infantrymen in the fighting for the northern Cotentin had begun to add skill and experience to the undoubted bravery shown earlier in the campaign, and were becoming, progressively, ever more effective fighters.

US soldiers relaxing in the aftermath of the Cherbourg surrender. From the towns and villages mentioned on the German-constructed signpost, the location of the photograph is east of the main port basins and towards the town of Tourlaville, adjacent to the modern ferry port. (*USNA*)

The main German line from Gruchy south was breached after heavy fighting and Lt Col Keil was captured at midnight on 30 June/1 July. Seventh Army headquarters had its final telephone communication with Battle Group *Keil* at around 2130 hours. US VII Corps headquarters considered that, 'An indication of the morale [of German units in this vicinity] generally was the speed with which the white flag was allegedly raised when thought [sic] that Lt Col Keil had been hit by shell fire.' The fighting here is covered in more detail as part of Tour D (*see pages 174–84*).

Interestingly, as the Americans moved ever westwards along the length of the peninsula the Germans began employing long-range artillery, based at the Blücher battery in the Channel island of Alderney, to shell their advance. Even at this stage, 30 June, German headquarters were still unsure about the exact position in Cherbourg, although intelligence suggesting the arrival of 50 Allied vessels was presumed to indicate that the naval batteries scattered along the coast were now at last out of action. The guns in the Landemer region, however, had been reported as shelling enemy shipping just the previous day. Even as late as this German Seventh Army was reporting that, 'We may assume that the remaining parts of Battle Group *von Schlieben* are defending themselves within the city, dealing out heavy losses to the enemy.'

THE ATTACKS TO THE SOUTH

Having successfully captured Cherbourg the American forces in the Cotentin turned their attention to the south. At the end of June, First US Army held a line that ran from Portbail/St-Lô-d'Ourville in the west, east towards Carentan and from there south-east as far as the town of Villiers-Fossard, just north of the key road and rail junction in the city of St-Lô. From there the American line ran roughly east as far as Bérigny before turning south to encompass Caumont and a link-up with the British Second Army sector west of Villers-Bocage. The American desire to push south had been put on hold while Cherbourg was taken for the simple reason that what the British termed the 'great storm' of 19–21 June had caused a widespread shortage of supplies, especially ammunition. As a result, sufficient resources simply did not exist to enable the American forces in France to pursue two major objectives simultaneously.

Eisenhower's choice of subsequent avenues of advance was twofold: either move directly east to strike at the major French cities of le Havre and Rouen, along the River Seine; or attack to the south with the intention of securing Brittany and St-Nazaire, Lorient and Brest. The US official history considered that, 'a move to the Seine ports, a more direct thrust towards Germany, was the bolder course of action, but unless the Germans were already withdrawing from France or at the point of collapse, success appeared dubious.' The capture of the Breton ports by US forces was also in line with the idea that US supplies would eventually come direct from the United States, rather than *via* Britain, and these ports, facing the Atlantic, were best placed to facilitate this. With these considerations in mind it was a relatively straightforward decision to advance south especially in concert with the impending Anglo-Canadian attacks south from their lodgement areas towards Caen on the River Orne.

Three separate and possible axes of advance, all along major arterial roads, marked the route south out of the Cotentin. The first was the road from la Haye-du-Puits to Coutances, almost

30 km to the south; the second from Carentan south-west to Périers. The third ran south from Carentan towards St-Lô. The route that Lt Gen Bradley intended to follow was the coastal one from la Haye-du-Puits to Coutances. The American plan to push out of the Cotentin peninsula was therefore as follows. VIII Corps, which had not participated as a corps in the fighting for Cherbourg and was comparatively fresh, was to advance through the small town of la Haye-du-Puits and from there to Coutances further south. The other American corps were to advance also, with VII Corps, fresh from its triumph at Cherbourg, to progress on the south-westerly route from Carentan to Périers while the (comparatively) recently landed XIX Corps was to push south from Carentan to St-Lô. Lt Gen Bradley, under considerable pressure to attack as soon as possible, made the decision to launch his three corps in separate advances with each corps attacking in turn, beginning with VIII Corps in the west. 'Battle Zone Normandy' *Battle for St-Lô* details the attacks of VII and XIX Corps but the initial push by VIII Corps south towards la Haye-du-Puits is covered below.

As the American official history points out so well, the German defenders at the base of the Cotentin were quite confident that they could hold out against the American drive. This confidence was not grounded in an overall appraisal of the respective economic and military might available to each side but more simply in the difficult terrain of the area. The American focus in the aftermath of the D-Day landings upon the seizure of Cherbourg, and the German focus on ensuring that whatever Allied forces came ashore remained in the Cotentin, had allowed the German defenders precious time to establish a coherent defensive position and they awaited the inevitable American push south with some confidence.

The US official history summed up the position.

'... despite the excellent defensive preparation... and utilizing the terrain to advantage... holding the line in Normandy was a gamble. As Rundstedt and Rommel had pointed out, if the Allies succeeded in penetrating the German positions, the absence of defensive lines between Normandy and the German border meant that the Germans would have to withdraw from France.'

Source: Martin Blumenson, *Breakout and Pursuit*, p. 50.

A burnt-out US vehicle, possibly an M8 Howitzer Motor Carriage, on the road to la Haye-du-Puits, 9 July. *(USNA)*

The attack of VIII Corps to the south had, as its objective, the aim of securing an operationally vital piece of land near Coutances. The initial target was the area of comparatively low-lying ground south-east of la Haye-du-Puits and facing the small town of Périers. VIII Corps, under Maj Gen Troy Middleton, aimed to deploy three battle-tested divisions, 79th Infantry Division in the west, 82nd Airborne Division in the centre and the previously troublesome 90th Infantry Division. The plan was for the two infantry divisions to converge south of la Haye-du-Puits with 82nd Airborne Division (due to return to England soon) tasked with a limited objective in the middle of the wedge. The paratroopers were due to be replaced by 8th Infantry Division. The success of VIII Corps' attack in the west was key to the American advance across the whole front, as this thrust would threaten the left flank of the German position south of the Cotentin.

The US plan was for the three divisions of VIII Corps to seize the high ground around la Haye-du-Puits and form a 'horseshoe' shape. 90th Infantry Division was handed the most difficult objective, the capture of Mont Castre in the east. In the centre

A relaxed-looking Maj Gen Ira 'Billy' Wyche, commanding officer of the 79th 'Cross of Lorraine' Infantry Division. Wyche eventually led the 79th into Germany as the first of the Western Allied units to cross into the Reich. *(USNA)*

82nd Airborne Division was tasked with securing the Poterie ridge and the high ground at Hill 131, some 3.5 km north-east of la Haye, with 79th Infantry Division taking the Montgardon ridge south-west of the town and Hill 121 (3 km west of Hill 131). The next stage of the attack called for 79th Infantry Division to head south as far as Lessay, 7 km south of la Haye, and then halt while momentum was maintained to the east by 90th Infantry Division in combination with the 8th Infantry Division, which was expected to have arrived by that juncture. The initial German assessment of the US activity was that it was no more than a 'major reconnaissance thrust' on the part of the Americans. This conclusion was hastily altered after the scale of the advance became apparent and, after some comparatively rapid US advances, German resistance stiffened appreciably.

At 0515 hours on 3 July the US forces attacked. Eisenhower had earmarked numerous Allied aircraft to support the attack, telling Middleton's staff that 'you can get all you want'. The night of the attack, however, saw heavy rain falling which prevented any air support whatsoever over the next few days.

In the centre of VIII Corps' attack, 82nd Airborne Division encountered mixed results. 505th and 508th PIRs made rapid progress, with the 505th successfully taking the north and east slopes of the key Hill 131 by mid–morning on 3 July, and the 508th securing the south-east slope of that same hill. These two regiments took very few casualties and such was the pace of their advance that many German units were by-passed, unaware of the attack. 325th GIR, the most easterly of 82nd Airborne Division's units, also pushed on rapidly for 2 km before being halted by heavy German fire directed from the area of Mont Castre, a substantial ridge that averaged 90 metres in height and extended for 5 km, west to east. Next, the 325th advanced to the eastern extremity of the Poterie ridge allowing the 505th and 508th to attack the German positions along what were termed the 'triplet hills' of the Poterie Ridge from the north. Heavy and confused fighting during the next two nights, with many US airborne troops finding themselves in the midst of German positions when dawn came, eventually saw the Poterie ridge secured by the afternoon of 5 July. 82nd Airborne Division had advanced 6 km during this period and suffered heavy casualties from determined German defenders fighting from well-prepared positions. 325th GIR entered the battle with 55 officers and 1,245 men and lost 14 officers and 289 men in a little over three days. The German view was rather different. The German forces facing 82nd Airborne Division included elements of *Ost Bataillon Huber* and German Seventh Army considered that, 'the decisive factor in the enemy breakthrough, in the opinion of the Army, was the inferior fighting qualities of the *Ost* battalions.'

War correspondents interviewing a captured *Wehrmacht* soldier in the devastated streets of la Haye-du-Puits on 11 July. The 'German' is in fact a soldier from an *Ost* battalion, many of whom surrendered to the Americans willingly, given the opportunity. *(USNA)*

On the western edge of the VIII Corps' position the experienced 79th Infantry Division made its attack with the Montgardon ridge, overlooking la Haye-du-Puits, as the initial objective. The highest point, Hill 84, was 2 km south-west of la Haye. *En route* to the ridge, the division was also to secure Hill 121, just west of

505th PIR's objective of Hill 131. The 314th Infantry attacked Hill 121 advancing along the road towards la Haye with two rifle companies leading the way, one on each side of the road. After initially being held up by German fire, the leading battalion of the 314th secured a position to the south of Hill 121 while a second battalion moved in behind and attacked from the south-west, securing the hill by mid-morning on 4 July. The 314th had advanced to within 3 km of the town by dusk on the 4th and also linked up with elements of 82nd Airborne Division.

315th Infantry Regiment, attacking the Montgardon ridge, made only slow progress after being surprised by concealed German vehicles that had been by-passed by the regiment's leading units. By the end of 3 July, the 315th had progressed about 1.5 km beyond its start line positions and by the end of 4 July the advance had closed to within 3.5 km of the top of the ridge at Hill 84. The successful capture of Hill 121 had allowed its height to be used to good effect by US artillery spotters and their work aided the advance of 315th Infantry Regiment.

In the early evening of 4 July the leading units were on the receiving end of a German counter-attack that employed several armoured vehicles in support of infantry. The artillery observers on Hill 121 reacted swiftly and, despite some early German success in isolating the forward American units, the Germans could claim only that the American advance had been halted rather than driven back.

A brief foray by 314th Infantry Regiment into la Haye-du-Puits was driven back on 5 July and 313th Infantry Regiment was brought into the attack with the intention of outflanking the ridgeline to the west. This move, although bold, did not succeed in changing the picture of the battle. Beginning its advance at noon on 5 July, 313th Infantry Regiment had not reached the ridgeline by late afternoon and two successive German counter-attacks drove the 313th backwards. A renewed effort by 315th Infantry Regiment late on 5 July, supported by the 314th and the 313th, led to the eventual American capture of the Montgardon ridge and Hill 84. The American position atop the ridge, and overlooking la Haye-du-Puits, looked to be strong. On 7 July, however, the Germans attacked in strength, with a force of approximately two battalions, with armour and artillery, in a devastating and unexpected counter-attack that came close to driving 79th Infantry Division from its hard-won position.

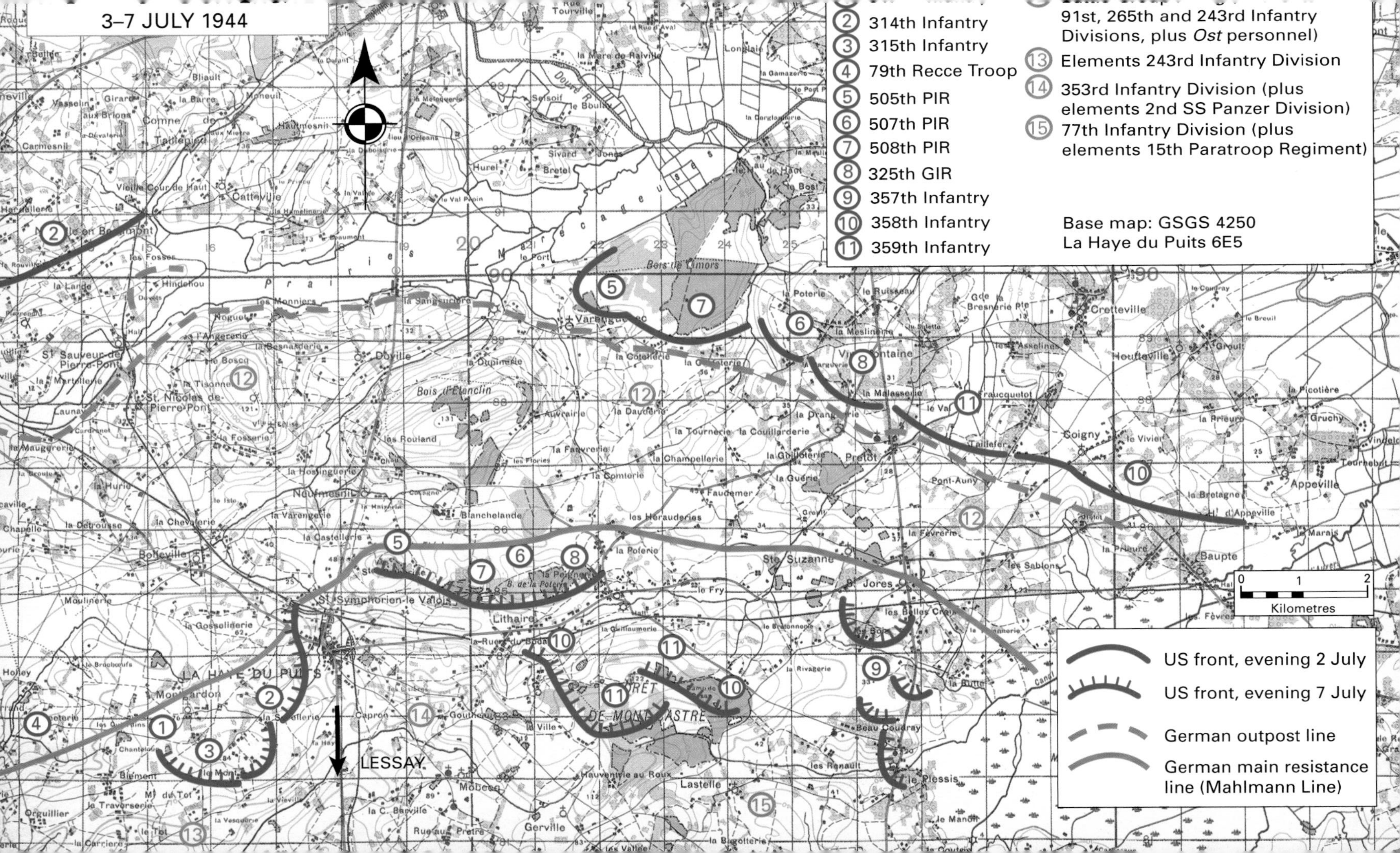
3–7 JULY 1944
2 314th Infantry
3 315th Infantry
4 79th Recce Troop
5 505th PIR
6 507th PIR
7 508th PIR
8 325th GIR
9 357th Infantry
10 358th Infantry
11 359th Infantry
91st, 265th and 243rd Infantry Divisions, plus *Ost* personnel)
13 Elements 243rd Infantry Division
14 353rd Infantry Division (plus elements 2nd SS Panzer Division)
15 77th Infantry Division (plus elements 15th Paratroop Regiment)
Base map: GSGS 4250
La Haye du Puits 6E5
0 1 2
Kilometres
US front, evening 2 July
US front, evening 7 July
German outpost line
German main resistance line (Mahlmann Line)
LA HAYE DU PUITS
LESSAY
Bois de Limors
Bois d'Etenclin
FORÊT DE MONT CASTRE
St Sauveur de Pierre-Pont
St. Nicolas de Pierre-Pont
St Symphorien-le Valois
Ste Suzanne
St Jores
Varenguebec
Vesly
Doville
Cretteville
Houtteville
Coigny
Appeville
Baupte
Pretot
Lithaire
Gerville
Bolleville
Neufmesnil
Blanchelande
Montgardon
Cattteville
Hautmesnil
Bretel
Prairies
Marecageuses

79th Infantry Division's Maj Gen Wyche combined 313th and 315th Infantry Regiments under a single officer (the commander of the 313th) in an attempt to strengthen the command and control on the ridge and stabilise the situation. The defence responded to this more coherent organisational arrangement and managed to resist the German attack.

Meanwhile, on the eastern edge of VIII Corps' advance, 90th Infantry Division was to be handed a golden opportunity to banish the question marks that had hung over it since the fighting for Cherbourg two weeks earlier. The seizure of the imposing Mont Castre ridge was a substantial task for the division. Mont Castre offered a contrast in terrain across its length. Although bare and sparsely covered with vegetation to the west, its eastern portion was very densely wooded and offered innumerable good defensive positions.

90th Infantry Division's war diary commented on the terrain.

'A marked feature of the forest of Mont Castre was the presence of thick underbrush so dense and of such height as to render movement slow and difficult, and to reduce visibility to little more than a few metres. Officers who participated called it more like jungle fighting than ordinary fighting in woods.'

Source: RG 407, Box 24206, ML 1070, US National Archives.

90th Infantry Division's commanding officer, now Maj Gen Eugene Landrum, planned to employ two of his infantry regiments, the 359th and the 358th, in the initial assault, with 357th Infantry Regiment held in reserve, ready to pass through and drive on to the initial objective of VIII Corps to the north-east of Lessay. 359th Infantry Regiment was tasked with securing the high ground of Mont Castre and advancing to the south-west, there to link up with 79th Infantry Division in its drive. 358th Infantry Regiment's objective was to push through the narrow gap between the eastern edge of Mont Castre and the north-western extremes of the Prairies Marécageuses de Gorges, the low-lying wetlands that dominated the southern Cotentin. Landrum hoped then to send in 357th Infantry Regiment to exploit the initial US success.

At 1200 hours on 4 July, US First Army celebrated Independence Day by firing every available gun across its entire front. According to Lt Gen Bradley's memoirs, 1,100 pieces were involved. Here Bradley himself participates by pulling the lanyard of a 155-mm howitzer at noon on the 4th. *(USNA)*

Although Landrum's reasoning was sound, the execution of the action proved more difficult. After some initially rapid progress, 90th Infantry Division proved unable to make headway against stiff opposition and by nightfall on 3 July had suffered 600 casualties in advancing about 1.5 km. 358th Infantry Regiment had its advance impeded by German armour for much of the day, only for the actual strength of the Germans to be revealed as a solitary assault gun and two half-tracks. A lack of determination in the leading battalion appears to have been responsible, at least in part, as well as inexperience in combining infantry and tanks in combat conditions. 359th Infantry Regiment also made little progress from its initial start positions and on 4 July, after a second day of hard fighting but little real progress towards its objectives, 90th Infantry Division took in excess of the 600 casualties suffered the day before. The overwhelming impression of the fighting was of the few German defenders using what weapons and positional advantages they possessed extremely well while the American attackers continued to demonstrate a reluctance to go forward except in the most favourable of circumstances. The judgement on the men of 358th Infantry Regiment (cited in Martin Blumenson *Breakout and Pursuit*) was that most 'seemed primarily concerned with taking cover in their slit trenches', although towards the end of 4 July the regiment did manage to make some progress towards the vital ground between les Prairies and Mont Castre. The only consolation for Landrum was that he was undoubtedly whittling away the numbers of German defenders, who were already stretched thinly. However, Landrum's forces could not continue to take casualties on such a scale either. On 5 July, 358th Infantry Regiment was withdrawn, judged 'too depleted and too weary for further offensive action' and replaced by the fresh 357th.

Refugees make way for US armour near la Haye-du-Puits, 14 July. *(USNA)*

While 357th Infantry Regiment, too, struggled to advance in the corridor, much as the 358th had done, on the right flank of the divisional advance 359th Infantry Regiment finally made progress against the slopes of Mont Castre. A break in the weather allowed Allied airpower to make an impression and this, together with well co-ordinated and concerted artillery and infantry action, saw the 359th, plus a battalion of the 358th, atop Mont Castre at last and in possession of its highest point, Hill 122. Constant local German counter-attacks throughout the night of 6 July never allowed the Americans to rest nor to consolidate adequately their hard won gains. By the morning of 7 July, however, it was apparent that the Germans had probably exhausted themselves in trying to regain the high ground. 357th Infantry Regiment, meanwhile, successfully moved into the corridor and advanced towards Beau-Coudray, holding positions to the north by 7 July.

Over the course of these four days of heavy fighting 90th Infantry Division had taken 2,000 casualties. The official verdict on the division's performance was remarkably even-handed, emphasising the comparative strength of the German defenders (who came mainly from 77th and 91st Divisions), the difficulty of the mission and the terrain that favoured the German defenders. The 90th Infantry Division's attacks had obliged LXXXIV Corps to deploy all its reserve formations and for German Seventh Army, too, to expend reserve forces in halting the US advance. Overall, however, 90th Infantry Division had again disappointed, aside from 'displaying workmanship and stamina' during the battles for the high ground of Mont Castre.

Tired and dirty US infantry moving south from la Haye-du-Puits on 9 July. *(USNA)*

The VIII Corps' plan had envisaged that 90th and 79th Infantry Divisions would meet south of la Haye-du-Puits, pushing beyond 82nd Airborne Division in the centre and, in doing so, allowing this unit to withdraw from combat and return to England. By dusk on 7 July VIII Corps was some way from being able to achieve this with the advance elements of the two infantry divisions still some 5 km apart. With the three divisions having suffered on average 15 per cent casualties during the previous four days of fighting, the corps commander,

A tired US mortar team take what rest they can on 8 July, after hard fighting in and around la Haye-du-Puits. The soldier in the foreground is cradling a German MP40 sub-machine gun, obviously a souvenir of the recent battles. (*USNA*)

Maj Gen Middleton, decided to introduce his fresh 8th Infantry Division and to change the lines of advance of 79th and 90th Infantry Divisions, with 82nd Airborne Division finally withdrawing. 8th Infantry Division would take over the corps' main effort, securing a bridgehead over the Ay River between Lessay and Périers. 79th Infantry Division was to take la Haye-du-Puits while 90th Infantry Division changed its direction of attack from south-west to south-east, eventually to give way to VII Corps on the division's eastern flank.

On 8 July, 79th Infantry Division attacked la Haye-du-Puits with tanks, artillery and tank destroyers in an effort to overwhelm the German defenders, rumoured to be only of company strength but well dug-in within a comprehensively mined defence perimeter. 79th Infantry Division made appeals to the German defenders in la Haye-du-Puits to surrender but with no success. The assault battalion, 1/314th Infantry, supported by B Company, 749th Tank Battalion, struggled to cross the extensive minefields and suffered many casualties from well-concealed German positions before moving slowly into the town centre, clearing the defenders house by house.

The 314th Infantry Regiment's war diary gave a detailed description of the defences.

'The perimeter defences of the town consisted of an extensive system of trenches reminiscent of World War I. The trenches were all connected to a central control tower... the trenches were protected in front by barbed wire entanglements, innumerable mines and booby traps.'

Source: 79th Infantry Division history; RG 407, Box 24053, Folder 153, US National Archives.

At midday on 9 July the town was turned over to 8th Infantry Division. 8th Infantry Division, also known as the 'Pathfinder Division', although highly recommended, suffered many problems in what was literally its baptism of fire. 8th Infantry Division units were routinely seen to be disorganised and incapable of seizing the initiative when local German weaknesses offered ample opportunities to do so. Among other complaints the green unit was accused of 'inaccurate reporting of map locations, large numbers of stragglers and poor employment of attached units'. The death on 10 July of the division's widely respected second-in-command, Brig Gen Nelson Walker, proved to be the last straw for Middleton and he relieved 8th Infantry Division's commanding officer, Maj Gen William McMahon, of his post. The change of command, and the knowledge that comes with prolonged experience, saw 8th Infantry Division evolve into a useful fighting force, living up to its pre-deployment reputation.

Order of Battle: 8th Infantry Division

10 July 1944

Commanding General:	***Maj Gen William C. McMahon***
Assistant Div. Commander:	*Brig Gen Nelson M. Walker*
Artillery Commander:	*Brig Gen James A. Pickering*

Organic Units

13th Infantry Regt	*Col Robert A. Griffin*
28th Infantry Regt	*Lt Col Henry B. Kunzig (acting)*
121st Infantry Regt	*Col John R. Jeter*

8th Reconnaissance Troop; 12th Engineer Combat Battalion;
28th Field Artillery Battalion (155-mm howitzer);
43rd, 45th, 56th Field Artillery Battalions (105-mm howitzer)

Attached Units

86th Chemical Weapons Battalion

Cherbourg harbour in the middle of August 1944, some six weeks after its capture. An American locomotive is arriving for use on the French railways. US Army engineers charged with clearing up the port employ the services of a specialist 'crane ship' to do the work normally carried out by static cranes on the harbour-side. *(USNA)*

90th Infantry Division was also building on its achievements and on 11 July 358th Infantry Regiment finally cleared the remaining German defenders from the high ground of Mont Castre, the 357th at last clearing the village of Beau-Coudray. The division continued to take heavy casualties as it pushed further south through the hedgerows until halting at the River Sèves. By 14 July VIII Corps had reached a line north of the Lessay–Périers axis after 11 days of hard fighting and high casualties through the narrow lanes of the Normandy *bocage*. Only now did its opponent, LXXXIV Corps, begin to withdraw south of the Sèves and Ay Rivers, having exhausted all its reserves. The original VIII Corps objective, the key city of Coutances, was still more than 22 km away and would not be taken until after the successful capture of St-Lô by XIX Corps.

The Allied advances in Normandy, while slow, were irresistible. The 'Battle Zone Normandy' volumes concerning the subsequent battles, entitled *Battle for St-Lô* and *Operation Cobra* pick up the story where this book finishes. If the reader wishes to find out more about these events then these two volumes are invaluable.

PART THREE

BATTLEFIELD TOURS

GENERAL TOURING INFORMATION

Normandy is a thriving holiday area, with some beautiful countryside, excellent beaches and very attractive architecture (particularly in the case of religious buildings). It was also, of course, the scene of heavy fighting in 1944, and this has had a considerable impact on the tourist industry. To make the most of your trip, especially if you intend visiting non-battlefield sites, we strongly recommend you purchase one of the general Normandy guidebooks that are commonly available. These include: *Michelin Green Guide: Normandy*; *Thomas Cook Travellers: Normandy*; *The Rough Guide to Brittany and Normandy*; *Lonely Planet: Normandy*.

TRAVEL REQUIREMENTS

First, make sure you have the proper documentation to enter France as a tourist. Citizens of European Union countries, including Great Britain, should not usually require visas, but will need to carry and show their passports. Others should check with the French Embassy in their own country before travelling. British citizens should also fill in and take Form E111 (available from main post offices), which deals with entitlement to medical treatment, and all should consider taking out comprehensive travel insurance. France is part of the Eurozone, and you should also check exchange rates before travelling.

GETTING THERE

The most direct routes from the UK to Lower Normandy are by ferry from Portsmouth to Ouistreham (near Caen), and from Portsmouth or Poole to Cherbourg. Depending on which you choose, and whether you travel by day or night, the crossing takes between four and seven hours. Alternatively, you can sail to Le Havre, Boulogne or Calais and drive the rest of the way. (Travel time from Calais to Caen is about four hours; motorway

Above: The French First World War memorial beneath Cherbourg's Fort du Roule. (*Author)*

Page 107: Corporal David Halberg, a Signal Corps photographer, allegedly the first US soldier to enter Valognes, looks around for snipers, 21 June. *(USNA)*

and bridge tolls may be payable depending on the exact route taken.) Another option is to use the Channel Tunnel. Whichever way you decide to travel, early booking is advised, especially during the summer months.

Although you can of course hire motor vehicles in Normandy, the majority of visitors from the UK or other EU countries will probably take their own. If you do so, you will also need to take: a full driving licence; your vehicle registration document; a certificate of motor insurance valid in France (your insurer will advise on this); spare headlight and indicator bulbs; headlight beam adjusters or tape; a warning triangle; and a sticker or number plate identifying which country the vehicle is registered in. Visitors from elsewhere should consult a motoring organisation in their home country for details of the documents and other items they will require.

Normandy's road system is well developed, although there are still a few choke points, especially around the larger towns during rush hour and in the holiday season. As a general guide, in clear conditions it is possible to drive from Cherbourg to Caen in less than two hours.

Accommodation

Accommodation in Normandy is plentiful and diverse, from cheap campsites to five star hotels in glorious châteaux. However, early booking is advised if you wish to travel between June and August. Useful contacts include:

French Travel Centre, 178 Piccadilly, London W1V 0AL; tel: 0870 830 2000; web: www.raileurope.co.uk

French Tourist Authority, 444 Madison Avenue, New York, NY 10022 (other offices in Chicago, Los Angeles and Miami); web: www.francetourism.com

Calvados Tourisme, Place du Canada, 14000 Caen; tel: +33 (0)2 31 86 53 30; web: www.calvados-tourisme.com

Manche Tourisme; web: www.manchetourisme.com

Maison du Tourisme de Cherbourg et du Haut-Cotentin, 2 Quai Alexandre III, 50100 Cherbourg-Octeville; tel: +33 (0)2 33 93 52 02; web: www.ot-cherbourg-cotentin.fr

Gîtes de France, La Maison des Gîtes de France et du Tourisme Vert, 59 Rue Saint-Lazare, 75 439 Paris Cedex 09; tel: +33 (0)1 49 70 75 75; web: www.gites-de-france.fr

In Normandy itself there are tourist offices in all the large towns and many of the small ones, especially along the coast.

Private John Wilczewski shaves in his foxhole, prior to the final Cherbourg offensive. *(USNA)*

BATTLEFIELD TOURING

Each volume in the 'Battle Zone Normandy' series contains from four to six battlefield tours. These are intended to last from a few hours to a full day apiece. Some are best undertaken using motor transport, others should be done on foot, and many involve a mixture of the two. Owing to its excellent infrastructure and relatively gentle topography, Normandy also makes a good location for a cycling holiday; indeed, some of our tours are ideally suited to this method.

In every case the tour author has visited the area concerned recently, so the information presented should be accurate and reasonably up to date. Nevertheless land use, infrastructure and rights of way can change, sometimes at short notice. If you encounter difficulties in following any tour, we would very much like to hear about it, so we can incorporate changes in future editions. Your comments should be sent to the publisher at the address provided at the front of this book.

To derive maximum value and enjoyment from the tours, we suggest you equip yourself with the following items:

- Appropriate maps. European road atlases can be purchased from a wide range of locations outside France. However, for navigation within Normandy, the French Institut Géographique National (IGN) produces maps at a variety of scales (www.ign.fr). The 1:100,000 series ('Top 100') is particularly useful when driving over larger distances; sheet 06 (Caen – Cherbourg) covers most of the invasion area. For pinpointing locations precisely, the current IGN 1:25,000 Série Bleue is best (we use extracts from this series for the tour maps in this book). The sheets required for the area discussed in this book are *1210 OT Cherbourg*, *1310 OT Cherbourg*, *1211 OT Les Pieux*, *1211 E St-Sauveur-le-Vicomte*, *1212 ET La Haye-du-Puiits – Lessay* and *1312 O Périers*. These can be purchased in many places across Normandy. They can also be ordered in the UK from some bookshops, or from specialist dealers such as the Hereford Map Centre, 24–25 Church Street, Hereford HR1 2LR; tel: 01432 266322; web: <www.themapcentre.com>. Allow at least a fortnight's notice, although some maps may be in stock.
- Lightweight waterproof clothing and robust footwear are essential, especially for touring in the countryside.
- Take a compass, provided you know how to use one!

- A camera and spare films/memory cards.
- A notebook to record what you have photographed.
- A French dictionary and/or phrasebook. (English is widely spoken in the coastal area, but is much less common inland.)
- Food and drink. Although you are never very far in Normandy from a shop, restaurant or *tabac*, many of the tours do not pass directly by such facilities. It is therefore sensible to take some light refreshment with you.
- Binoculars. Most officers and some other ranks carried binoculars in 1944. Taking a pair adds a surprising amount of verisimilitude to the touring experience.

SOME DO'S AND DON'TS

Battlefield touring can be an extremely interesting and even emotional experience, especially if you have read something about the battles beforehand. In addition, it is fair to say that residents of Normandy are used to visitors, among them battlefield tourists, and generally will do their best to help if you encounter problems. However, many of the tours in the 'Battle Zone Normandy' series are off the beaten track, and you can expect some puzzled looks from the locals, especially inland. In all cases we have tried to ensure that tours are on public land, or viewable from public rights of way. However, in the unlikely event that you are asked to leave a site, do so immediately and by the most direct route.

A 4th Armored Division soldier browses through the official French phrasebook issued to troops, Barneville, July 1944. *(USNA)*

In addition: **Never remove 'souvenirs' from the battlefields.** Even today it is not unknown for farmers to turn up relics of the 1944 fighting. Taking these without permission may not only be illegal, but can be extremely dangerous. It also ruins the site for genuine battlefield archaeologists. Anyone returning from France should also remember customs regulations on the import of weapons and ammunition of any kind.

Be especially careful when investigating fortifications. Some of the more frequently-visited sites are well preserved, and several of

A US medical team administer blood plasma to a German prisoner wounded during the march on Cherbourg, 26 June 1944. Major David J. Weaver (holding the plasma bottle) directs the operation. *(USNA)*

them have excellent museums. However, both along the coast and inland there are numerous positions that have been left to decay, and which carry risks for the unwary. In particular, remember that many of these places were the scenes of heavy fighting or subsequent demolitions, which may have caused severe (and

Montebourg town centre. Even after the destruction wrought on the town during its liberation more was yet to come. Here US Army engineers rest in between their efforts to bulldoze a path through the rubble (and occasional intact buildings) to clear a supply route for the advance to Cherbourg. *(USNA)*

sometimes invisible) structural damage. Coastal erosion has also undermined the foundations of a number of shoreline defences. Under no circumstances should underground bunkers, chambers and tunnels be entered, and care should always be taken when examining above-ground structures. If in any doubt, stay away.

Beware of hunting (shooting) areas (signposted *Chasse Gardée*). Do not enter these, even if they offer a short cut to your destination. Similarly, Normandy contains a number of restricted areas (military facilities and wildlife reserves), which should be avoided. Watch out, too, for temporary footpath closures, especially along sections of coastal cliffs.

If using a motor vehicle, keep your eyes on the road. There are many places to park, even on minor routes, and it is always better to turn round and retrace your path than to cause an accident. In rural areas avoid blocking entrances and driving along farm tracks; again, it is better to walk a few hundred metres than to cause damage and offence.

In addition to the above, various points specific to this volume should be raised.

By their very nature these tours frequently traverse areas that are not well catered for in terms of restaurants and/or *tabacs*. It is

recommended, therefore, that tourers come prepared with adequate supplies or food and drink and assume that refreshments will not be generally available. Where possible, suitable restaurants and shops are named in the following tours. The author has visited all of the restaurants mentioned, in the course of research for this part of the book and all (at the time of writing!) are recommended as being both of a good quality as well as reasonably priced.

The following tours are all focused upon the efforts of the United States Army's VII Corps, under the command of Maj Gen 'Lightning Joe' Collins, to capture the major port city of Cherbourg. For the purposes of the tours, it is assumed that the city of Cherbourg will be the main base for any tourers. However, Cherbourg itself is a rather utilitarian port, a useful jumping-off point, but not generally a destination in its own right.

Tour C follows the American advance from the south into the heart of Cherbourg and the Fort du Roule and includes a visit to the *Musée de la Liberation*, but in addition to this there are other sites within the city which are related to the 1944 battles. These include General von Schlieben's command bunker and the old Naval Arsenal.

The probable location of GenLt von Schlieben's command post is under this concrete bunker in the St-Sauveur suburb of Cherbourg. (*Author*)

The US Advance into Cherbourg
26 June 1944
1 47th Infantry Regiment
2 39th Infantry Regiment
3 12th Infantry Regiment
4 313th Infantry Regiment
5 314th Infantry Regiment
6 315th Infantry Regiment
Base map: IGN 1210OT
a Entrance to Naval Arsenal
b Probable location of von Schlieben's command bunker
c Cherbourg town hall
d Cherbourg central railway station
e Gare Maritime (Cité de la Mer)
f First World War memorial
g 'Cherbourg' sign
h Cherbourg Liberation Museum
Port Chantereyne
Patinoire
Rue de l'Abbaye
La Bucaille
Boulevard Guillaume le Conquérant
Val de Saire
Boulevard P Mendès France
Avenue J-F Millet
St-Sauveur
Rue de Président Loubet
Rue St. Sauveur
Rue Barthélemy Picquerry
Avenue de Paris
Avenue E Lecarpentier
Amont-Quentin
Villa Rocca
les Provinces
N 2013
0
0.5
1
Kilometres

German troops, waving a large and very visible white flag, emerge from GenLt von Schlieben's command bunker, 26 June 1944. *(USNA)*

The location of von Schlieben's bunker is undramatic when reached as little is now visible of the below-ground complex from which he tried to direct the battle for Cherbourg and from where he surrendered to US forces. To reach it head west from the SNCF station along the Boulevard Pierre Mendès-France, taking the sixth turning on the left, the Rue de President Loubet heading south-west up the hill into the St-Sauveur district, just to the south of the main town. At the top of the hill the Rue de President Loubet intersects with the Rue St-Sauveur. To the left of the crossroads formed by the junction of these two roads (almost due south) is a new development, the Residence Barthélémy.

After research in the Office of Naval History in Cherbourg, using their extensive wartime maps of German bunkers and their fate post-war, the author concluded that underneath these new buildings is the likely location of GenLt von Schlieben's command post. By continuing over the hill along the Rue Barthélémy Picquerry and taking the first turning to the left it is possible to see the structure shown in the photo on page 115. This looks like an entrance to an underground facility and is over the area where von Schlieben's bunker should be. Beyond that there is no definite proof but the probability is strong that this is the location.

Cherbourg Office of Naval History

Service Historique de la Marine à Cherbourg, 57 Rue de l'Abbaye, BP 31, 50100 Cherbourg-Octeville. Open 0900–1200 & 1330–1800 Mon–Thur, 0900–1200 & 1330–1700 Fri.

The Arsenal was the last bastion of concerted German resistance in Cherbourg and was commanded by the former commandant of the whole Cherbourg fortress, GenMaj Robert Sattler. Sattler's eventual surrender brought an end to the fighting in Cherbourg. The arsenal complex was spared a final and devastating bombardment and assault by US troops after Sattler decided to give up without a fight. Although access to the arsenal complex is not possible, tourers can walk around its length courtesy of a new cycling/walking path.

The high, thick walls of the Cherbourg naval arsenal. Fortunately the defenders chose to surrender rather than fight on. (*Author*)

No visit to Normandy, especially one that seeks to explore the role of the United States Army in the fighting, would be complete without a visit to one of the many war cemeteries in the region. In particular, given the focus of this book, the American cemetery at Colleville-sur-Mer, above Omaha Beach, certainly rewards a visit. From Cherbourg this can be reached in an hour or so by driving south-east along the N13 as far as Isigny and then following the coast road (D514), which runs through Grandcamp-Maisy to Omaha Beach and Colleville-sur-Mer. Most of the units involved in the fighting for Cherbourg, however, landed at Utah Beach on the eastern side of the Cotentin and this area is also recommended to the tourer.

OTHER ATTRACTIONS

For those wishing to combine their tours with a vacation that takes in the many and varied delights of Norman cuisine and culture there are few if any examples that cannot be found in greater numbers and greater depth beyond Cherbourg itself. Having said that, there are a number of interesting attractions in Cherbourg that are worth visiting even if one is based elsewhere.

Of particular note is the *Cité de la Mer*, which features a variety of 'sea-themed' exhibits including the deepest aquarium in Europe, and the ex-French Navy submarine *Le Redoutable*. This ballistic missile vessel was formerly a central element of France's *force de frappe* (nuclear deterrent) and is 'the world's largest submarine open to the public', although the interior is no longer original. It is worth mentioning that this exhibit does not admit children under six. *Cité de la Mer* is located in the old *Gare Maritime*, the former rail terminal for transatlantic liner passengers, which was thoroughly demolished by the Germans in 1944 before the American forces took the port.

Cherbourg's famous transatlantic liner terminal. All the major unloading berths along the left side of the terminal have been comprehensively destroyed and a scuttled ship is visible to the right, lying on its port side and effectively blocking any access to the deep water basins beyond. (*USNA*)

In Cherbourg one particular restaurant of note is the very good *Au Provencal*, serving pizzas and a variety of *specialités mediterranéenes*. It is in the central area of town at 27–29 Rue Tour Carée. In addition there are innumerable small cafés and fast food establishments near the main road to the ferry port. Cherbourg also has a number of large *supermarchés* in this area that seem to market themselves primarily to British travellers intent on taking advantage of France's lower alcohol prices; these can be accessed easily while *en route* to the ferry terminal beneath the Montagne du Roule.

Useful addresses

Cité de la Mer, Gare Maritime Transatlantique, 50100 Cherbourg-Octeville; tel: +33 (0)2 33 20 26 26; email: <courrier@citedelamer.com>. Open 0930–1900, 1 June–30 Sept; 1000–1800, 1 Oct–31 May. Closed 25 Dec, 1 Jan & 6–24 Jan. Last admission 1 hr before closing time. Admission charge

International Youth Hostel, 55 Rue de l'Abbaye, 50100 Cherbourg-Octeville 50100; tel: +33 (0)2 33 78 15 15; email: <cherbourg@fuaj.org>. Open 6 Jan–21 Dec.

Barneville-Carteret Tourist Office, 10 Rue des Écoles, BP 101, 50270 Barneville-Carteret; tel: +33 (0)2 33 04 90 58; email: <tourisme.barneville-carteret@wanadoo.fr>; web: <www.barneville-carteret.net>. Open 0900–1230 & 1400–1800 daily, except Sundays and festivals.

Colleville Military Cemetery, Omaha Beach, 14710 Colleville-sur-Mer; tel: +33 (0)2 31 51 62 00; web: <www.abmc.gov>. Open 0900–1700 daily, except 25 Dec and 1 Jan.

Being based near Cherbourg, rather than in the town itself, is not a problem as road links are generally good in the northern Cotentin. The author has visited the area over the course of a Bastille Day weekend and for several days before and after; even then the roads and beaches were still pleasantly under-used and progress was unhindered by traffic problems of any description.

Choices of accommodation in the Cotentin are extensive from inexpensive pensions and campsites to plusher hotels and self-catering villas. If one is interested in a no-frills stay in Cherbourg then the international youth hostel in Rue de l'Abbaye is ideal as it is very conveniently located for central Cherbourg (just minutes from *Cité de la Mer*) and the non-member tariff of 14 euros (summer 2003) includes a continental breakfast. The author stayed here for several nights in July 2003 and was pleasantly surprised by the quality of the rooms (four occupancy maximum, all *en suite*) and the general demeanour of the hostel, more akin to a smart budget hotel than the barebones approach of many hostels in years gone by. The main tourist office (*Maison du Tourisme*) in Cherbourg (details on page 110) is very useful and can offer advice on food, accommodation and other sites of interest in both Cherbourg and Normandy. Needless to say the staff there speak a multitude of languages. In Cherbourg generally, a function of its port status no doubt, English is spoken widely in contrast to the rest of the northern Cotentin.

In addition to the main cross-channel ferry services described earlier it is also possible to travel from the Channel Island of Jersey to Barneville-Carteret on the west side of the Cotentin. This is of particular interest here because Barneville is also the termination point of Tour A. The town of Barneville-Carteret runs a number of concert programmes and activities for families during the summer periods and is also well provided with camping facilities.

TOUR A

THE DRIVE TO BARNEVILLE

OBJECTIVE: This tour examines aspects of the American drive across the Cotentin peninsula which aimed to isolate Cherbourg and its German garrison, preventing their resupply and reinforcement and thereby facilitating the capture of Cherbourg's port facilities. It focuses upon the exploits of the three battalions of 60th Infantry Regiment (9th Infantry Division) as they moved westwards at considerable speed towards Barneville.

DURATION/SUITABILITY: The tour covers about 36 km and can be completed in half a day. Although moderately hilly, the tour proceeds through quiet countryside and is therefore suitable for cyclists. Tourers with mobility difficulties may find Stand A3 slightly difficult to access, although a reasonable view can be gained from the road near where the stand is located.

Stand A1: Camp Patton

DIRECTIONS: From Cherbourg drive south-west along the D3, turning south onto the D900 towards Bricquebec. At Bricquebec, continue on the D900 towards St-Sauveur-le-Vicomte. About 5 km south of Bricquebec, just beyond the small village of le Gros Chêne, turn left (east) on a minor road following the signs to 'Camp Patton' for approximately 300 metres.

To BRICQUEBEC
and CHERBOURG
0
1
2
Kilometres
D900
D42
Ste-Colombe
Néhou
St-Jacques-de-Néhou
River Douve
Bois de Denneville
Parc Naturel Régional
des Marais du Cotentin
NATUREL
le Mont
Golleville
Aureville
les Forges de Vardon
1 2/60th Infantry and elements 746th Tank Battalion, afternoon 16 June
2 Elements 2/60th Infantry, afternoon 16 June
3 Position held by E/60th Infantry, evening 16 June
4 Elements 82nd Airborne Division, evening 16 June
5 2/60th Infantry, morning 17 June
6 60th Infantry Regiment, 17 June
7 Position held by 1/39th Infantry, early morning 18 June
8 German breakout attempt, early morning 18 June

In the northern Cotentin peninsula, unlike the area inland from the landing beaches further east, there are few examples of military equipment on display to record the fighting of 1944. At Camp Patton, however, there is this well preserved M4 Sherman tank. *(Author)*

THE SITE: Strictly speaking, this diversion has no direct relevance to the cutting of the Cotentin peninsula; nevertheless, it has considerable historical interest in its own right. This is one of the initial locations used by Lt Gen George Patton's Third US Army headquarters, which moved from its base in England at the start of July 1944. Even though the Allies were ashore in Normandy in some strength, they were still maintaining Operation Fortitude (the deception plan to convince the Germans that the main Allied landings were still to come in the Pas de Calais area). To this end Patton's taking command of Third US Army was kept secret. The memorial at this location commemorates Patton's original HQ ('Lucky Forward') in Normandy, which was located in the orchard here. The memorial also includes some interesting

The orchard area at Camp Patton. This was the actual location of Patton's command post and this is commemorated by the standing stone and affixed metal plaque. *(Author)*

information relating to the actions fought in the Avranches area later in the Battle of Normandy.

Stand A2: The River Douve at Sainte-Colombe

DIRECTIONS: Retrace your route from Camp Patton to the D900. Turn left and head south towards St-Sauveur-le-Vicomte for 2 km. At les Forges de Vardon turn left (east) along the D42 for 4 km to Ste-Colombe, crossing the three bridges immediately west of the village. Turn around in Ste-Colombe and park at the hard standing opposite a small cottage, with the easternmost bridge now just ahead of you.

THE SITE: Stand by the nearest bridge looking west along the D42 towards the village of Néhou. Ahead of you is another bridge across the main course of the River Douve, while 250 metres beyond 'la Laiterie' (the dairy) a third bridge spans one of the river's tributaries. The successful capture of all three bridges was carried out by elements of the 2nd Battalion, 60th Infantry (9th Infantry Division) on the afternoon and evening of 16 June 1944. In the process they established an important bridgehead over the Douve, thus facilitating the American advance towards Barneville.

THE ACTION: The successes of the 9th Infantry and 82nd Airborne Divisions in their respective attacks westwards on 15 June 1944 prompted Maj Gen Collins' announcement that 'the major effort of the [VII] Corps is now to cut the [Cotentin] peninsula'. Advancing from Reigneville the next day, Lt Col Michael B. Kauffman's 2/60th Infantry was the first unit to reach the small village of Ste-Colombe, with orders to secure a bridgehead across the River Douve. After sporadic fighting at the crossroads 2 km south-east of the village, during which several Germans were killed and 17 captured, the battalion occupied the village at about 1530 hours. Led by E Company and some Sherman tanks from 746th Tank Battalion's B Company, it then continued west towards Néhou.

The Americans rapidly seized the first two bridges across the Douve, but when they reached the third they found it damaged. Unable to cross, the tanks turned back, leaving many of the infantry strung out along the causeway linking the bridges.

Simultaneously, accurate German artillery and small arms fire began to fall among the US troops, causing considerable confusion and some panic. Although E Company managed to establish itself on the west bank (initially on the eastern edge of Néhou; later on a small knoll about 750 metres south-east of the village), its supporting machine-gun platoon and F Company fell back in disorder into Ste-Colombe.

The approach to the third of the crucial bridges that span the River Douve and its minor tributaries at Ste-Colombe. The picture is taken looking west, in the direction of the American advance. The retreating Germans damaged this bridge in 1944; the current bridge is of a more modern, post-war design. *(Author)*

Although the American bridgehead seemed highly vulnerable, there appear to have been few Germans in the immediate area, and despite persistent shelling no counter-attacks were launched. Anxious to report his gains, Kauffman set off to the divisional command post, where he was instructed by a delighted Maj Gen Collins to maintain his position until reinforcements (3/60th Infantry) arrived. Kauffman then returned to Ste-Colombe in a 2½-ton truck loaded with ammunition, which he drove across all three bridges to the forward positions held by E Company. Soon afterwards, a machine-gun platoon succeeded in crossing the river to provide further assistance, and by midnight the beleaguered 2nd Battalion had been reinforced by further elements of 60th Infantry Regiment. As a result, the American position astride the River Douve was secured.

Stand A3: Hill 145

DIRECTIONS: Retrace your route from Ste-Colombe across the three bridges that span the Douve and drive along the D42 as far as St-Jacques-de-Néhou, some 7 km in all. Continue west along the D42 for a further 3 km to the crossroads with the D50 at la Croix Pelletier. Continue straight ahead (still on the D42), but after approximately 800 metres turn right onto a minor road. After 500 metres, at the T-junction with the D242, turn left towards Grand Hameau and St-Pierre-d'Arthéglise. Follow this road west for roughly 3 km until just past Hameau des Chasses Mauger. The first turning right leads to Hill 145, which was captured by 2/60th Infantry late on 17 June (Hill 133, occupied by 1/60th Infantry at the same time, is immediately south of the D242 in the same general area). Follow the road uphill for about 800 metres, bearing right on each occasion you encounter a junction, until you reach a wartime bunker on the right, and park on the hard standing adjacent to what appears to be a water-pumping station (shown as two small circles just south of Point 145 on the tour map). The bunker, which judging by its insignia and other features was a *Luftwaffe* command post, is an interesting site in itself, although for some reason it is not marked on modern French maps.

The *Luftwaffe* bunker near the summit of Hill 145. The *Luftwaffe* eagle insignia is very clear above the main entrance door, though the swastika has been chiselled off in a crude fashion. (*Author*)

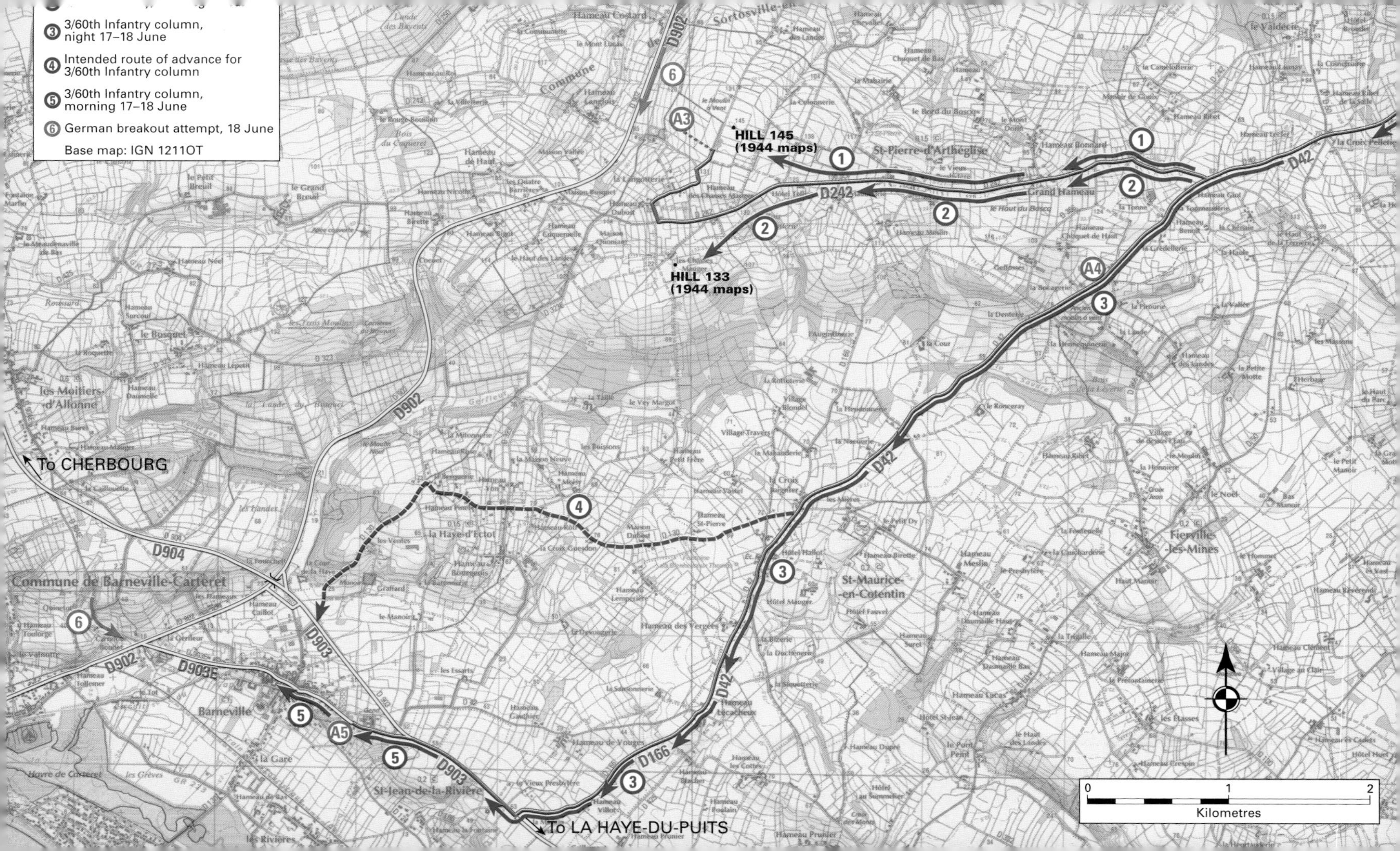
3 3/60th Infantry column, night 17–18 June
4 Intended route of advance for 3/60th Infantry column
5 3/60th Infantry column, morning 17–18 June
6 German breakout attempt, 18 June
Base map: IGN 1211OT
HILL 145 (1944 maps)
HILL 133 (1944 maps)
St-Pierre-d'Arthéglise
Grand Hameau
St-Maurice-en-Cotentin
Fierville-les-Mines
Barneville
St-Jean-de-la-Rivière
Commune de Barneville-Carteret
les Moitiers-d'Allonne
To CHERBOURG
To LA HAYE-DU-PUITS
D42
D242
D902
D903
D903E
D904
D166
A3
A4
A5
Kilometres
0
1
2

The view afforded to US troops after having secured Hill 145. This picture looks west and at the left, slightly to the right of the lone telegraph pole, can be seen the curve of the Bricquebec–Barneville road. On this road the retreating German columns were subject to murderous US artillery fire from guns positioned close to the point from which this picture was taken. (*Author*)

After inspecting the bunker, return to the road. Walk uphill for approximately 100 metres until a narrow track is apparent on your left. Walk along this track into the field about 200 metres away and face west.

THE SITE: Looking west into the valley you can see the D902 heading south-west from Bricquebec to Barneville. Behind you is Hill 145, occupied by 2/60th Infantry late on the 17th. Using forward observers emplaced on this feature, guns from 60th Field Artillery Battalion were able to strike mercilessly at German columns withdrawing south along the D902 the following day.

THE ACTION: At 0600 hours on 17 June, 60th Infantry Regiment moved to capitalise on its success in securing a bridgehead at Ste-Colombe. Heading west through Néhou, which the Germans had abandoned in the night, the regiment advanced to St-Jacques-de-Néhou, which was seized during the afternoon, and then towards the small village of St-Pierre-d'Arthéglise. About 2 km west of this village lay high ground dominating the

surrounding countryside as far as the coastal town of Barneville, the main objective on the western side of the peninsula for the northern element of the cross-Cotentin drive. Significantly, this position also overlooked the main road linking Barneville and Bricquebec. The 60th Infantry rapidly moved west in battalion columns astride the main road, encountering no large scale, organised resistance, save for isolated incidents with various 'straggler' units. One of these, a German artillery battalion (according to the US official history, but more likely a battery) was captured intact by 1/60th Infantry during its advance to Hill 133.

Although its personnel were very tired, the rapid progress made by 60th Infantry Regiment encouraged Maj Gen Collins to instruct 9th Division not to halt, but to cut the peninsula overnight. Consequently, at some point during the evening Maj Gen Eddy made his famous comment, 'We're going all the way tonight', to members of the 60th Regiment's headquarters, arrayed along the road near St-Jacques-de-Néhou. As a result, the 1/60th and 2/60th pushed through to their respective objectives, Hill 133 and Hill 145. Here, the following day, they encountered considerable German forces as the latter attempted to break through the American positions and thus escape from the inevitable US encirclement.

The biggest engagement occurred during the morning of 18 June, when a lengthy German column was observed west of Hill 145 moving south along the D902. These troops appear to have been from 77th and 243rd Infantry Divisions, as well as a variety of other LXXXIV Corps units. Fired at by the 105-mm howitzers of 60th Field Artillery Battalion, the mixture of horse-drawn and motor vehicles was soon brought to a halt. The US artillery fired first at the head of the German column before working its way north for several kilometres along the road. According to subsequent inspection, 35 trucks, half-tracks and cars were destroyed, as well as 10 artillery pieces, one tank and numerous other vehicles.

Later, 60th Artillery Battalion's guns were obliged to move when their position was threatened by other German attempts to escape south, this time further east, north of St-Jacques-de-Néhou. These troops were engaged by men of 1st Battalion, 39th Infantry Regiment (Lt Col Tucker), which had been assigned to aid the 60th's advance west by covering its flanks to the north. After initially being forced back by fierce German attacks at 0430 hours on the 18th, at 0900 hours 1/39th Infantry counter-attacked with considerable artillery and mortar support. Driving north, the battalion pushed the Germans across the River Scye, about 2 km away, before halting. Some 250 Germans were reported killed, with another 60 captured. Among the German casualties, according to the US official history, was GenLt Rudolf Stegmann, commander of 77th Infantry Division, who was mortally wounded during a fighter-bomber attack in this area.

Maj Gen Manton S. Eddy, the tough commanding officer of US 9th Infantry Division, with an unknown German officer prisoner. Eddy, a professional soldier who had seen service in the First World War, demonstrated the importance of continuity in command, having led his division since 1942 through successive campaigns in Tunisia and Sicily before the fighting for Cherbourg. *(USNA)*

Stand A4: 9th Division memorial west of la Croix Pelletier

DIRECTIONS: Return to the D242 and drive east through St-Pierre-d'Arthéglise and Grand Hameau. Retrace your route all the way back to the D42, turning right (south-east) about 600 metres beyond Grand Hameau in order to do so. At the D42 turn right (west) again, and after another kilometre you will see a memorial to the right of the road; this is well marked thanks to the Tricolour and Stars and Stripes flying above the hedgerows, which are clearly visible some distance away. There is hard standing just beyond the memorial allowing easy parking.

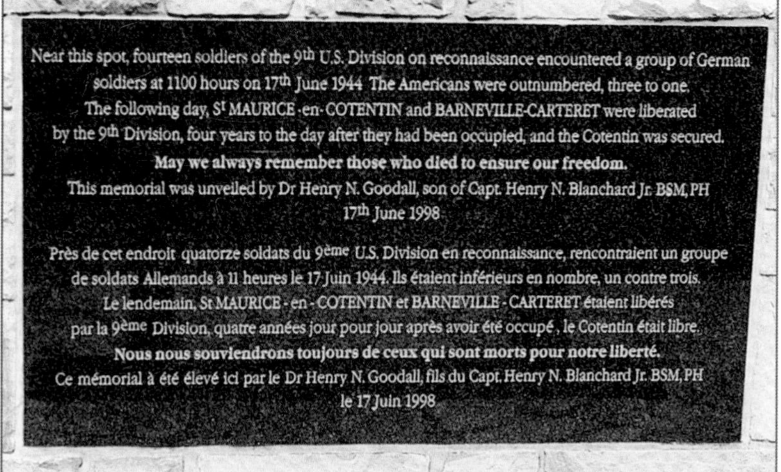

The inscription on the roadside memorial to men of the 9th Infantry Division, unveiled by the son of one of the US soldiers killed. *(Author)*

THE SITE: The 3rd Battalion, 60th Infantry, advanced along this road, the D42, to cut the peninsula at Barneville. This small and comparatively recent memorial (1998) commemorates their achievement. The major part of the inscription reads as follows:

> 'Near this spot, fourteen soldiers of the 9th US Division on reconnaissance encountered a group of German soldiers at 1100 hours on 17th June. The Americans were outnumbered three to one. The following day, St-Maurice-en-Cotentin and Barneville-Carteret were liberated by the 9th Division, four years to the day after they had been occupied, and the Cotentin was secured.'

No indication is provided regarding the identity of the unit to which the men mentioned in the inscription belonged, although it is possible, given the location of the memorial, that they were members of 3/60th Infantry. Further research in the US official histories and documentary sources did not (at the time of writing) reveal any more details about this incident. What it does serve to illustrate is the curious nature of the fighting in the middle Cotentin, where seeking always to push forward and seize the initiative against an enemy mostly, but not always, in retreat could result in running into opposing forces with local superiority and greater firepower.

The Barneville memorial commemorates the cutting of the Cotentin peninsula by 9th Infantry Division on 18 June 1944. *(Author)*

Stand A5: Barneville memorial

DIRECTIONS: Drive west along the D42 towards the village of St-Maurice-en-Cotentin. Pass through the village centre and continue for about 1 km as far as the junction with the D166 at Hameau Lecacheux, signposted to St-Jean-de-la-Rivière. Take the D166 through Hameau Villot before turning right onto the main Barneville-sur-Mer–la Haye-du-Puits road, the D903. Drive north-west towards Barneville for 900 metres and turn left onto the D903E, signposted to Barneville-Carteret. On the left 200 metres after this junction there is a large monument to the cutting of the peninsula, along with an excellent view of the town of Barneville-Carteret (these two neighbouring communities having merged since 1944). Park where it is safe to do so.

THE SITE: The route that you have just followed is the one taken by 3/60th Infantry and its accompanying armoured vehicles from 746th Tank Battalion and 899th Tank Destroyer Battalion on the night of 17–18 June. This composite force advanced from the vicinity of la Croix Pelletier, west of St-Jacques-de-Néhou, and headed down the main road (now the D42) towards St-Maurice. Confusion in the darkness, however, saw the column continue south through Hameau Villot, rather than swinging west as intended to move into Barneville from the north. As a result the force approached the town from the high ground to the south-east.

> **Accounts of this diversion, provided by officers of 3/60th Infantry, indicate the fickle hand of fate apparent in wartime.**
>
> 'This change of route was quite unintentional, but turned out to be a fortunate error for the Germans were moving to Barneville, some of them possibly knowing of our drive in that direction, and the enemy was found throughout this area of the main highway the next day! No opposition [however] was encountered on the march to Villot.'
>
> *Source:* 9th Infantry Division combat interviews; RG 407, Box 24026, Folder 53, US National Archives.

THE ACTION: The 3rd Battalion, 60th Infantry, advanced down the D42 with its K Company leading, riding atop five Sherman tanks belonging to B Company, 746th Tank Battalion, four tank destroyers (from A Company, 899th Tank Destroyer Battalion) and four half-tracks of the anti-tank platoon. L and I Companies followed on foot, with M Company (heavy weapons) travelling in its own transport. The column was commanded by Captain (later Major) Keene Wilson, who had taken over the battalion at la Croix Pelletier when the previous CO was diagnosed as suffering from exhaustion and evacuated.

After 'jumping off' from la Croix Pelletier at 2200 hours on 17 June, 3/60th Infantry made good progress. Despite a two-hour hold up caused by a single anti-tank gun about 2 km north of St-Maurice-en-Cotentin, the formation reached Hameau Villot at 0200 hours on 18 June. After avoiding German troops mounted on bicycles near Villot the battalion then advanced towards Barneville, arriving by 0500 hours at the spot marked by the monument.

Although the town looked empty, it was clearly necessary to occupy it in order to be sure. This move was carried out by 1st Lieutenant Williamson's K Company, with armoured and heavy machine-gun support. Although Barneville seemed quiet when K Company entered, and only a few surprised German military policemen were rounded up, according to the account of Major Wilson and other officers, 'Fifteen minutes later Germans seemed to appear from all directions, some attempting to get back into the town. Luckily they didn't all attempt to enter the town at the same time.' Sporadic fighting then continued throughout the day as the Americans captured German soldiers in Barneville and then successfully engaged small columns attempting to move through the town to the south, the Germans unaware that US forces had both secured Barneville and cut the road to la Haye-du-Puits. A particularly prominent role was played by the tank destroyers under the command of Lieutenant Coady, although I, L and M Companies also fought hard from their blocking position (near the present-day monument) to prevent the enemy from escaping, and US aircraft also provided welcome support.

The major encounter of the day occurred at 1000 hours when around 125 German troops counter-attacked from the south-east. This attack was beaten off by L Company and 85 prisoners taken. Although some German troops did succeed in percolating through US lines during the following 48 hours, by the evening of 18 June the Cotentin peninsula had effectively been cut in two. The advance to Cherbourg could now begin in earnest.

A German officer reports on the consequences of the American breakthrough to Barneville for his own unit.

'On 17 June, the 77th Infantry Division and the 3rd Battalion [243rd Artillery Regiment] were ordered to attempt to bypass the enemy who had advanced to St-Jacques-de-Néhou and to fight their way through to the German lines in the south. The whole day had to be passed in waiting, on account of the clear weather and the

An aerial view of the town of Barneville, the westernmost objective of US efforts to sever the Cotentin peninsula. This picture was taken at 400 feet (120 metres) on 28 July 1944 over a month after Barneville fell to US forces. *(USNA)*

strong enemy air activity... As the battalion now had three prime movers for seven guns, the 177th Artillery agreed that the battalion should move two guns by truck in the afternoon, in spite of the air attacks. They were moved to Barneville...

The quick advance of the enemy on Barneville led to the loss of the two guns delivered there, as well as of one horse-drawn gun... The crews belonging to these guns, who had been instructed to blow up their weapons in case of need, were likewise missing, with the exception of one man who, separated from his comrades, made his way through the enemy lines a few days later. Near Barneville a truck with food, including a bookkeeper and three cooks, was captured by the enemy after a fierce struggle. A truck fully loaded with ammunition that had been left standing behind the enemy lines on account of engine trouble, was fetched in the following night by assault detachments.'

Source: Report on 3rd Battalion, 243rd Artillery Regiment, (6–25 June 1944) by *Leutnant* Staalhofer; Appendix G to MS B-845, 'The German 709th Division during the fighting in Normandy', US National Archives.

TO CONCLUDE THE TOUR: To return to Cherbourg rejoin the D903 (which becomes the D904 immediately north of Barneville) and drive north. Alternatively, if you wish to linger, Barneville-Carteret is a pleasant and unspoiled beach town. The small beachside restaurant of *l'Orchide*, literally on the seafront, serves generous and reasonably priced local *moules* and is thoroughly recommended.

TOUR B

HILL 158 AND THE OSTECK

OBJECTIVE: This tour examines the efforts of 22nd Infantry Regiment (4th Infantry Division) to isolate Cherbourg from the east. It examines the cutting of the key Cherbourg–Barfleur road, the capture of the airfield near Maupertus-sur-Mer, and the fighting around the large fortified position known as the *Osteck*.

The impressively straight D901 road as it heads west towards Tourlaville and Cherbourg, taken from a point north of Hill 158, which overlooks the road. All traffic moving between Cherbourg and the eastern Cotentin had to use this road. The D901 has been widened and straightened in the post-war period but still follows the same route, on this stretch, as it did in June 1944. *(Author)*

Maupertus airfield flak defences
Battery Hamburg
Cap Lévi radar station
Battery Seeadler
Osteck
Maupertus airfield (1944 perimeter)
Base map: IGN 1310 OT
For further details of the extensive
rman defences within this area, see the
944 Allied intelligence map on p.144
Cap Lévi
To BARFLEUR
Commune de Fermanville
D116
To BRETTEVILLE and CHERBOURG
Maupertus-sur-Mer
Aérodrome de Cherbourg-Maupertus
Hamel es Ronches
To ST-PIERRE-ÉGLISE and BARFLEUR
OURLAVILLE CHERBOURG
D901
D612
*POINT 158 (1944 maps)
D320
To LE THEIL
Gonneville
Carneville
0
0.5
1
Kilometres

It also provides information about the Hamburg coastal battery, located south of Cap Lévi in the Commune de Fermanville, and offers a good opportunity to explore the beautiful coastal region east of Cherbourg.

DURATION/SUITABILITY: This tour covers around 17 km and lasts about half a day. The terrain includes a number of hills, but is suitable for cyclists. Tourers with mobility difficulties, however, may wish to reach Stand B3 by vehicle using the track running through the centre of the *Osteck* position, rather than by the footpath suggested in the directions.

Stand B1: Hill 158

DIRECTIONS: From central Cherbourg drive east along the D901 through Tourlaville. (In 1944 Tourlaville was far more of a distinctly separate town than today. Now the transition from Cherbourg to Tourlaville is almost seamless save for the roadside signs that indicate when Tourlaville is reached.) Continue east for about 4 km after leaving Tourlaville to the junction with the D320 at le Rendez-Vous des Chasseurs, a few houses scattered along the main highway. Turn right onto the D320 and continue for 900 metres before taking the second turning on the left, which heads north-west back towards the D901. Continue up this track to the water pumping station on the right, parking on the hard standing nearby.

THE SITE: To your right, beyond the low concrete buildings, can just be seen the top of Hill 158, the highest point along the plateau east of Cherbourg (unusually, wartime and modern maps agree on this spot height). To the north is the D901, the main arterial route connecting Cherbourg with the airfield at Maupertus and the east coast of the Cotentin. The track you have just driven up is the route of advance for elements of 3rd Battalion, 22nd Infantry Regiment, on 21 June 1944.

THE ACTION: Following the German withdrawal into Fortress Cherbourg on the night of 19–20 June, VII Corps moved steadily towards its objective. In the east, Maj Gen Raymond O. Barton's 4th Infantry Division pushed forward to a line running north-east from the Bois de Roudou. After a largely unopposed 13-km

The small water pumping station and various aerials that cluster near the high point of Hill 158. This picture looks east to the actual summit. *(Author)*

advance, by nightfall on 20 June Colonel Hervey Tribolet's 22nd Infantry Regiment reached the area of le Theil, 4 km south-east of this stand. Here it came under fire from the high ground to the north, which caused heavy casualties among 1st Battalion as it struggled to establish a position along the banks of the River Saire (in this area, no more than a creek).

The following day, 22nd Infantry was ordered to continue the attack from its overnight positions to sever the main east–west road (now the D901) leading from Cherbourg eastwards past the airfield at Maupertus. The regiment's principal objective was Hill 158, 2 km west of Gonneville, which dominated the road and the surrounding countryside, and upon which a tall radio tower (according to one source, the main communications facility for the defences east of Cherbourg) was located. The 1st and 3rd Battalions, supported by the Sherman tanks of Company B, 70th Tank Battalion, led the advance. This force moved off at 1600 hours on 21 June and, with supporting artillery fire, advanced as far as the slopes north of Hameau Pinabel, 1 km south-east of Hill 158, after four hours. At this point the German defenders (from 30th Flak Regiment) began to lay down a hail of fire from anti-aircraft guns, bringing 1/22nd Infantry's advance to a halt. Nevertheless, 3/22nd managed to push on to the objective, which it reached before midnight.

The view north from the track leading past Hill 158. *(Author)*

Lt Col Arthur S. Teague, commanding 3/22nd Infantry, describes the methods used by the German anti-aircraft gunners at Hill 158.

'In this position and in the subsequent attack on the airport, the [3rd] Battalion suffered severely from fires of enemy 40-mm AA guns. These were being emplaced behind cover and elevated to fire the quick fuse shells, detonating on striking the slightest foliage. When the shells passed over the top of a hedgerow they would burst causing heavy casualties among men in the shelter of the hedgerow.'

Source: Interview (3 July 1944) with Lt Col Teague, 4th Infantry Division combat interviews; RG 407, Box 24014, Folder 29, US National Archives.

The two American battalions, although relatively secure in their existing positions, now found themselves increasingly isolated by German troops infiltrating across their lines of communication to the south. Some of these moves, which appear to have originated from the defences around Gonneville and the airfield, were in company strength. Supply convoys moving up through the narrow lanes, much akin to the one you are now standing in, were attacked on several occasions. On the morning of 22 June one such column was hit by machine-gun and artillery

fire and forced to turn back, while another convoy took a wrong turning and was ambushed on a narrow trail between high hedges, losing two light tanks, three half-tracks, three 57-mm guns and several jeeps. Partly for this reason, plans to use 22nd Infantry to support 12th Infantry Regiment in the latter's intended advance to Tourlaville had to be postponed on 22 June.

Anxious to secure their gains before launching the attack into Cherbourg from the east, the Americans decided to clear all German resistance from the area of Hill 158. In sporadic fighting on 22–23 June, 2/22nd first cleared the rear of 3/22nd Infantry's position on the hill itself, before sending combat patrols 2 km south to mop up resistance near Hameau Cauchon. Meanwhile part of 24th Cavalry Squadron, supported by B Company, 801st Tank Destroyer Battalion, and 4th Reconnaissance Troop, screened the area south of the airfield, and tanks pushed towards Gonneville. With the 22nd Infantry's 1st and 3rd Battalions consolidating on Hill 158, by the evening of 23 June the American position was much improved. As a result, late the same day 2/22nd was attached to 12th Infantry Regiment, which was tasked with attacking Tourlaville. On 24 June, while the rest of the regiment patrolled the high ground and kept the resupply routes open, 2/22nd assisted parts of 3/12th Infantry in capturing the heavily defended position at Digosville, 3 km south-west of Hill 158. Simultaneously, the rest of 12th Infantry established itself on the slopes overlooking Tourlaville, in preparation for an assault into the eastern part of Cherbourg the next day. On 25 June, as part of a general drive forward by 4th Infantry Division, 2nd and 3rd Battalions, 22nd Infantry, advanced to the coast east of Tourlaville, clearing the village of Bretteville. Meanwhile, 1/22nd remained in occupation of the Hill 158 area.

Stand B2: Maupertus airfield and the memorial to the US Ninth Air Force

DIRECTIONS: From your position on Hill 158, retrace your route to the D320 and back to the D901. At le Rendez-Vous des Chasseurs turn right onto the D901 and head east for 2.75 km. At the cluster of airport buildings west of Hamel ès Ronches, turn left at the sign for the Cherbourg/Maupertus airfield. Follow the road around to the right and stop adjacent to the memorial to the USAAF's Ninth Air Force.

The post-war administration building at Maupertus airfield. The airfield itself has also grown quite considerably since the war. In the foreground is the small memorial to the United States Army Air Force's Ninth Air Force. *(Author)*

THE SITE: Looking south from the memorial and the airport building approach road it should be possible to see, between you and the D901 and slightly obscured by undergrowth, a partially buried German bunker. Judging by wartime maps, this is part of the extensive anti-aircraft defences that ringed Maupertus airfield in June 1944.

THE ACTION: The German positions east of Hill 158 ran in a rough line north from the village of Gonneville as far as Cap Lévi, and included the Cherbourg airfield at Maupertus as well as the elaborate and extensive fortified complex known as the *Osteck*, on the high ground due north of this stand. By late June these positions were held by a mixture of army, navy, air force and other personnel, of which the most important elements were 30th Flak Regiment and the remnants of *Kampfgruppe Rohrbach* (729th Grenadier Regiment and attached units). In addition, the powerful 'Battery Hamburg' (9th Battery, 260th Naval Artillery Detachment), with four 240-mm (9.4-inch) guns and a garrison of several hundred naval and flak personnel, was located about 1.5 km north-east of the *Osteck*. Owing to the design of this battery, however, the Germans were unable to bring its main armament to bear against the US forces advancing from the south.

As described at Stand B1, the period 22–25 June saw 22nd Infantry Regiment holding positions in the area of Hill 158, protecting the right flank and rear of 12th Infantry Regiment's advance to Tourlaville. However, with the successful penetration into Cherbourg, by the evening of 25 June the regiment was available to turn its attention to the remaining German positions towards the north-east. Consequently, late that day Maj Gen Barton issued Colonel Foster with orders to mop up German resistance as far east as St-Pierre-Église and as far north as the tip of Cap Lévi.

The attack began on 1100 hours on 26 June, and involved all three battalions of 22nd Infantry Regiment, supported by 44th Field Artillery Battalion, the Shermans of 70th Tank Battalion and of a troop of cavalry on each flank. Despite heavy fire from flak guns, 1/22nd overran the defences south of the airfield and captured Gonneville. Meanwhile 2/22nd occupied the western edge of the airfield, north-west of where you are standing, and 3/22nd seized the village of Maupertus and the airfield's northern perimeter. The whole area was then mopped up over the following 24 hours.

Stand B3: The Osteck

DIRECTIONS: Return to the D901 from the airport buildings and continue east for 1.75 km. At the eastern end of the airfield turn left onto the D612. Driving north, you are effectively passing along the eastern perimeter of the Cherbourg defences; a glance at the map overleaf reveals numerous German positions on both sides of this road. Most significant of all was Battery Hamburg, whose four concrete gun casemates can still be located beside the D612 near Hameau Carré.

THE ACTION: Although unable to interfere with the US advance from the south, on 25 June this Navy battery (plus a nearby Army 105-mm battery) participated in a furious duel with an Allied naval force under the command of Rear Admiral Morton L. Deyo, which was providing fire support for VII Corps' attack. In a five hour exchange, the battleship USS *Texas* succeeded in knocking out one of the German naval battery's guns by a direct hit with a 14-inch shell. However, Battery Hamburg succeeded in hitting not only the *Texas*, but also the

German defences east of Cherbourg, as plotted by the Allies in 1944, among them the *Osteck* and Battery *Hamburg* (upper right). Maupertus airfield, with its extensive flak defences, is at centre right. Battery *Seeadler*, unoccupied by 6 June, is clearly visible immediately south of the Pointe du Brulay (*sic*). The most recent intelligence is shown in red. *Base maps:* GSGS 4347 Cherbourg 31/22SW, St-Pierre-Église 31/22SE, Stop Press edition, 20 May 1944.

American destroyers *Barton*, *Laffey* and *O'Brien*. Fortunately for Admiral Deyo, most of the strikes turned out to be duds, no ships were sunk, and at 1501 hours the Allied task force retired.

The official history of US naval operations describes the moment when the USS *O'Brien* was hit by Battery Hamburg.

'Despite the feeling of *Texas*['s] sailors that their ship was the enemy's only target, they were getting comparatively small stuff; Hamburg's guns, strangely enough, were not [yet] firing at her, but concentrating on destroyers and minesweepers, then "churning about like loony ants" (as it seemed to the battleship's sailors) to evade. Hamburg's next victim was the destroyer *O'Brien*. At 1251 a shell sheared away the ladder to her bridge, scattered her signal flags over the deck, and caromed into the after corner of the combat information center. There, in the ship's nerve center, it exploded. Thirteen men were killed and 19 wounded. Her skipper, Commander Outerbridge, turned north immediately to investigate damage and found that all radar was out of commission. This was not pleasant, since her smoke screen, made to cover her retirement, was so dense that all other ships were out of sight. Like a blind man escaping a forest fire, *O'Brien* felt her way through the smoke to comparative safety in waters north of the approach channel.'

Source: S.E. Morison, *History of United States Naval Operations in World War II: The Invasion of France and Germany 1944–1945*, p. 209.

More information about the naval action on 25 June can be found at Stand D2, pages 173–4.

DIRECTIONS: After driving along the D612 for approximately 4 km you will reach the coast road, the D116. You may decide at this point to divert temporarily from the tour route to visit Cap Lévi, either to view the coastline or to inspect the remains of further German positions in this area (these can be located on the tour map). However, if you wish to proceed with the tour, turn left onto the D116 and head west for 2.5 km before parking on the left at the picnic site near the Pointe du Brûlé. From here walk up the hillside along the marked trail, which bends inland after about 250 metres. After another 200 metres you will arrive at a large and well-preserved German bunker, the observation post for the Army *Seeadler* ('Sea Eagle') battery, which originally was manned by 5th Battery, 1709th Artillery Regiment (709th Infantry Division). According to Allied intelligence, however, this position was unoccupied before D-Day, and it is unclear whether or not any guns were re-positioned here by late June.

The observation post for the *Seeadler* battery. Although defaced by graffiti, this bunker appears to have suffered very little Allied attention during the fighting for Cherbourg. Such battle damage as is apparent, however, is on the southern side, facing away from the sea, consistent with the US efforts to secure the massive *Osteck* complex from the south. *(Author)*

Looking inland towards the high ground 1 km distant you should be able to see several large scars in the otherwise uniformly green terrain. These gashes mark a modern motocross track, clearly indicated as such on most maps of the area. In fact the motocross track conceals the remains of several bunkers within the eastern lynchpin of the 'ring of steel' that surrounded Fortress Cherbourg: the *Osteck*.

To reach the *Osteck* continue walking south along the trail. After 300 metres the trail crosses another track, running east to west. Along this track, in four separate positions, are the gun emplacements of *Batterie Seeadler*. From the remaining physical evidence it appears that the guns here operated on turntables and that ammunition was brought up behind the gun pits (a crane apparatus remains behind one of the positions).

One of the *Seeadler* gun positions. Clearly visible here is the swivelling base mount for the gun. In 1944, however, there would have been no foliage to block the view of the sea to the north. (*Author*)

Proceed further uphill, joining the main track to the *Osteck* about 200 metres beyond the gun positions just mentioned. After a further 500 metres, stop in front of the motocross complex. This area is fenced in but is accessible through a gate to the north (left) of where you are standing. Obviously, the best time to visit is when a motocross meeting is not being held. What you are looking at are the remains of substantial German fortifications and bunker positions, partially destroyed in 1944 and further demolished during the 1950s. The area between the buildings has been filled in, in places, to improve the area's utility in its current function, and it is difficult to visualise the original configuration of the complex. Nevertheless, its formidable scale is still evident.

THE ACTION: The fighting to secure the *Osteck* involved both 1/22nd and 3/22nd Infantry, and climaxed on 27 June. The *Osteck* position had not received any recent communication with Cherbourg other than the sporadic reception of messages indicating that positions in the city itself were being surrendered. The outlying German forts were gradually overrun by US infantry and Sherman tanks, or shelled into submission by 44th Field Artillery Battalion, leaving only the main position in German hands. After capturing one bunker the US troops managed to secure a telephone line to the German commander, an artillery major named Friedrich Küppers (sometimes spelled

Kaupers). He was asked to surrender or face a combined air and artillery bombardment and further ground assaults. According to some accounts, despite having run out of artillery ammunition Küppers initially refused to capitulate, preferring to await the expiry of the deadline, early on the morning of 28 June.

The following morning the commander of 4th Infantry Division, Maj Gen Barton, himself spoke to Küppers under a white flag. Although he reminisced about his time as a young officer near Küppers' home town of Wiesbaden after the First World War, Barton's appeals appeared to be fruitless. However, when he revealed a detailed map of the *Osteck* complete with the names of the officers and senior NCOs responsible for its component parts, Küppers decided to give in. After the Germans' surrender it was noted that their positions possessed 'elaborate periscopes [which] covered all… of the peninsula to the coast and permitted numbers to be read on ships at sea.'

When asked for further specifics about what had persuaded him to surrender, Küppers simply said '[American] panzers to the right, panzers on the left, panzers in front, troops everywhere.' After this confession Küppers ordered all German troops nearby – among them the naval personnel at Battery Hamburg – to give themselves up and the Americans took almost a thousand prisoners. In addition Küppers ordered his men to de-mine the roads in the area.

The narrow track that runs behind (to the south) of the *Seeadler* gun positions. This picture of the most easterly position shows what appears to be an ammunition hoist for hauling the heavy shells up and into the gun pit itself. It is possible that a narrow gauge railway once ran along the track. *(Author)*

The view above the coast looking north from one of the higher points of the modern motocross track. On the coast in the far distance, in the middle of the picture, is the observation bunker at Pointe du Brûlé mentioned earlier. *(Author)*

Lt Col Teague describes his memory of the capture of the *Osteck*, giving a different account of the surrender.

'Captain Blassard went to the underground fortification and the commanding Major asked to see the Commanding Officer of the Battalion. Col. Teague received the Major's surrender at 2330 hours [on 27 June] and ordered the Major to order his 290 men out of the pillboxes and to show him where his lines were. Fort Hamburg was still firing on the airport [presumably, some of the flak guns protecting the Battery Hamburg complex, since the 240-mm pieces could not shoot in this direction] so it was decided to keep the men on the hill during the night. The prisoners requested that they be allowed to return to their bunkers for their blankets. Col. Teague refused... but allowed them to go to the mess hall [an underground facility with an alleged capacity of 500 men] and remain there for the night, unguarded. Major Kaupers [*sic*] was a "decent joe and he entertained the American officers with beer and cheese." Col. Teague said "he wanted to be nice to those guys because I wanted to be sure that the rest of [the] fortifications stayed surrendered and didn't start raising hell that night."'

Source: Interview with Lt Col Arthur S. Teague; RG 407, Box 24014, Folder 29, US National Archives.

What appears, judging by what remains, to be the main command bunker of the *Osteck*. The modern motocross track is clearly visible in this picture as it runs over the top of the bunker. *(Author)*

TO CONCLUDE THE TOUR: Retrace your steps downhill to your vehicle. To return to Cherbourg follow the D116 west into the city (this route passes the Fort des Flamands at the eastern extremity of the inner breakwater). Alternatively, if you have not already done so, you may wish to head east to explore Cap Lévi and the coast towards Barfleur.

TOUR C

ADVANCE ON CHERBOURG AND THE FORT DU ROULE

OBJECTIVE: This tour follows the advance by elements of the US 79th Infantry Division as they made the final assault on Fortress Cherbourg between 20 and 26 June 1944. It culminates in an examination of the dramatic capture of the Fort du Roule, which overlooked the entire town and port area.

DURATION/SUITABILTY: The tour involves travel along busy main roads and is unsuitable for cyclists, although an alternative route can be planned using the tour map. Tourers with mobility difficulties will undoubtedly find the walking route to Stand C4 very demanding to say the least, and may wish to seek assistance or go directly to the Fort du Roule museum after Stand C3. The full tour takes a day, including a break for lunch.

Stand C1: The Cherbourg Landfront

DIRECTIONS: From Cherbourg drive south towards Valognes along the N2013 and then the N13 (the Voie de la Liberté). Approximately 7 km south of Cherbourg turn right, off the main road, into the village of Délasse. The road into the village follows the route along which the Americans advanced (in the opposite direction) in 1944. At the crossroads in the centre of the village turn left onto the D56, crossing the bridge over the N13 and continuing east for about 2.5 km. Stop at the turning onto a minor road to the left, where six pentagonal symbols, indicating Second World War fortifications, are marked on the tour map (*overleaf*). These were identified by Allied intelligence in 1944 as a flak site and a minor defensive position. Another flak battery was located a few hundred metres east of the Château de Pannelier, which can also be located on the tour map.

THE SITE: You are now standing at the southern edge of the semi-circle of defensive positions that ringed Cherbourg in 1944 as part of the German *Landfront*.

THE ACTION: Following the successful cutting of the Cotentin peninsula on 18 June (*see Tour A*) the US VII Corps moved to secure the port city of Cherbourg. The assault on the city was three-pronged, with 9th Infantry Division moving in from the west, 4th Infantry Division from the east (*see Tour B*) and Maj Gen Ira T. Wyche's 79th Infantry Division from the south.

The 79th Division's role was to advance towards Cherbourg along the axis of the Valognes–Cherbourg highway, clearing positions astride the road as it moved north. The division's ultimate objective, however, was the high ground immediately south of the city, and especially the Montagne du Roule. Atop this feature, which offers unrivalled views of Cherbourg and

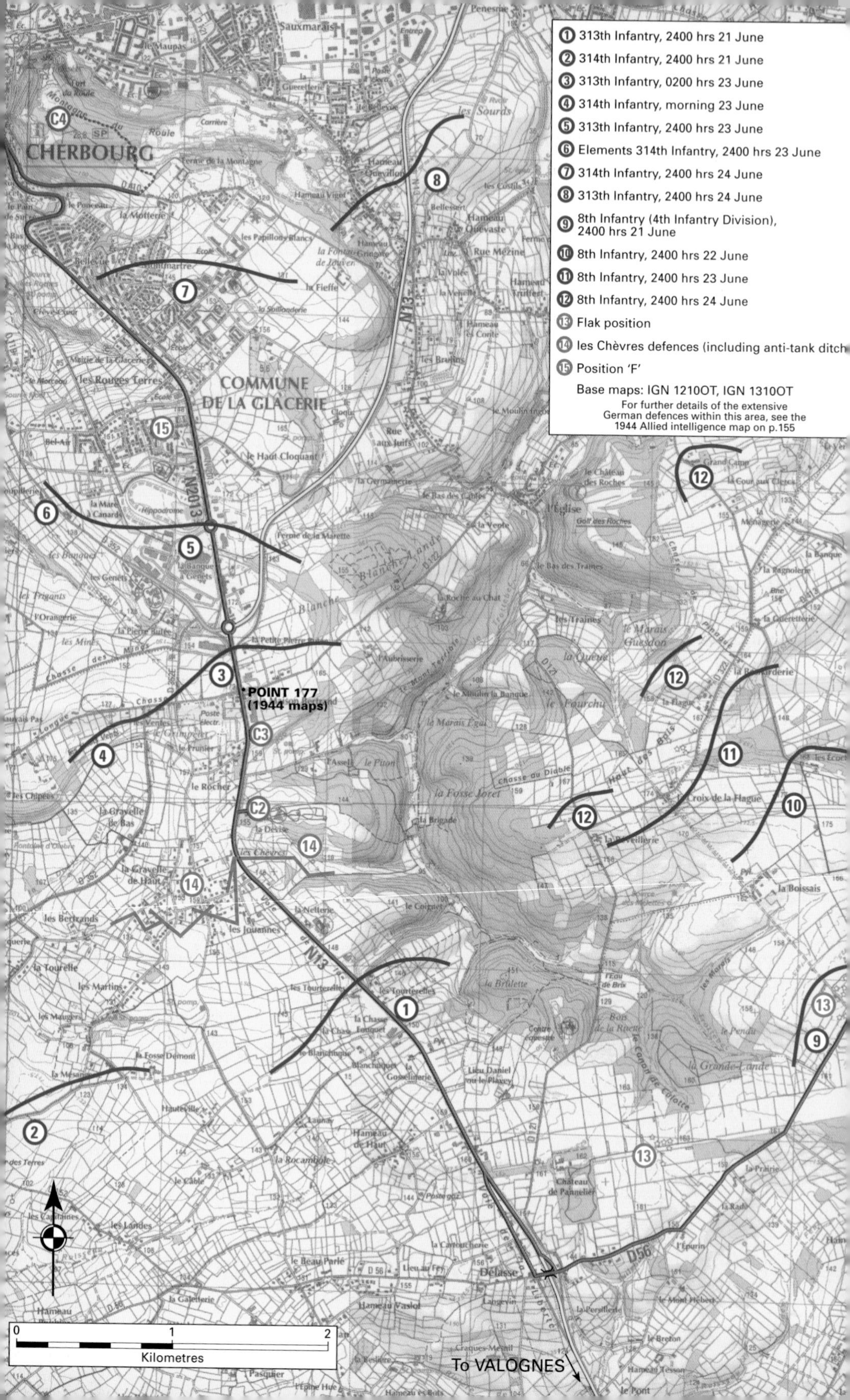

1 313th Infantry, 2400 hrs 21 June
2 314th Infantry, 2400 hrs 21 June
3 313th Infantry, 0200 hrs 23 June
4 314th Infantry, morning 23 June
5 313th Infantry, 2400 hrs 23 June
6 Elements 314th Infantry, 2400 hrs 23 June
7 314th Infantry, 2400 hrs 24 June
8 313th Infantry, 2400 hrs 24 June
9 8th Infantry (4th Infantry Division), 2400 hrs 21 June
10 8th Infantry, 2400 hrs 22 June
11 8th Infantry, 2400 hrs 23 June
12 8th Infantry, 2400 hrs 24 June
13 Flak position
14 les Chèvres defences (including anti-tank ditch
15 Position 'F'
Base maps: IGN 1210OT, IGN 1310OT
For further details of the extensive German defences within this area, see the 1944 Allied intelligence map on p.155
CHERBOURG
COMMUNE DE LA GLACERIE
POINT 177 (1944 maps)
C4
C3
C2
N13
N2013
D56
To VALOGNES
0
1
2
Kilometres

which dominates the skyline above the city and the sea approaches from the north, stood the formidable Fort du Roule.

After failing to cut the Valognes–Cherbourg road on 19 June, the 79th Infantry Division struck north again early the following day. Of its three infantry regiments, the 313th and 314th were to seize the highway and advance astride it towards Cherbourg. Meanwhile, the 315th Infantry Regiment would clear Valognes of any remaining opposition. Initial progress was good, with several German tanks and an 88-mm gun captured near St-Joseph, 4.5 km south-east of Délasse. Four US paratroopers, who had been in hiding since D-Day, were rescued by 2/314th Infantry, while 3/314th had the greatest success of the day, overrunning a V-2 rocket site 1 km south of Brix (this position is easily identifiable on the IGN 1:25000 scale map, sheet 1310 OT). Meanwhile, 313th Infantry Regiment's 2nd Battalion came under artillery and machine-gun fire on the main road, but managed to push forward to Délasse by nightfall. Here its patrols encountered the first defences of the *Landfront*, and the advance temporarily was called to a halt.

US troops at a captured V-1 launch site at la Sorellerie (Château Pannelier), 1 July. *(USNA)*

Stand C2: les Chèvres

DIRECTIONS: Retrace your route towards Délasse, rejoining the N13 just east of the village centre. Drive north for just over 5 km. As the road bends to the right look out for a right turn at a

sign advertising the camping site *le Village Vert*. Turn right here and park 100 metres along the road.

THE SITE: You are standing at the northern edge of the first major strongpoint identified during the 79th Division's advance on Cherbourg. The defences here were located on both sides of the main road, with a lengthy anti-tank ditch facing south and a number of bunkers, trenches and pillboxes behind it. The tactical advantages of the position can be seen by walking back to the main Valognes–Cherbourg highway and looking towards the restaurant on the far side of the dual carriageway.

From the stand there are commanding views to the south and east, as well as some evidence of the German defences beyond the *Defense: deposer des ordures* (no tipping) sign. By walking along the road to the camp site, and looking south where the hedgerows allow, you can easily see how German forces dug in at the top of several steep gullies could dominate any approach to Cherbourg from the south.

Looking to the south-east from the approximate site of the German position at les Chèvres. This area demonstrates the German aptitude for identifying the most appropriate ground for defensive positions. *(Author)*

THE ACTION: After a pause to regroup on 21 June, during which US patrols attempted to identify German resistance nests, on 22 June final preparations began for VII Corps' attempt to breach the defensive perimeter around Cherbourg. For the men of 79th Infantry Division the route into the city was to be from the

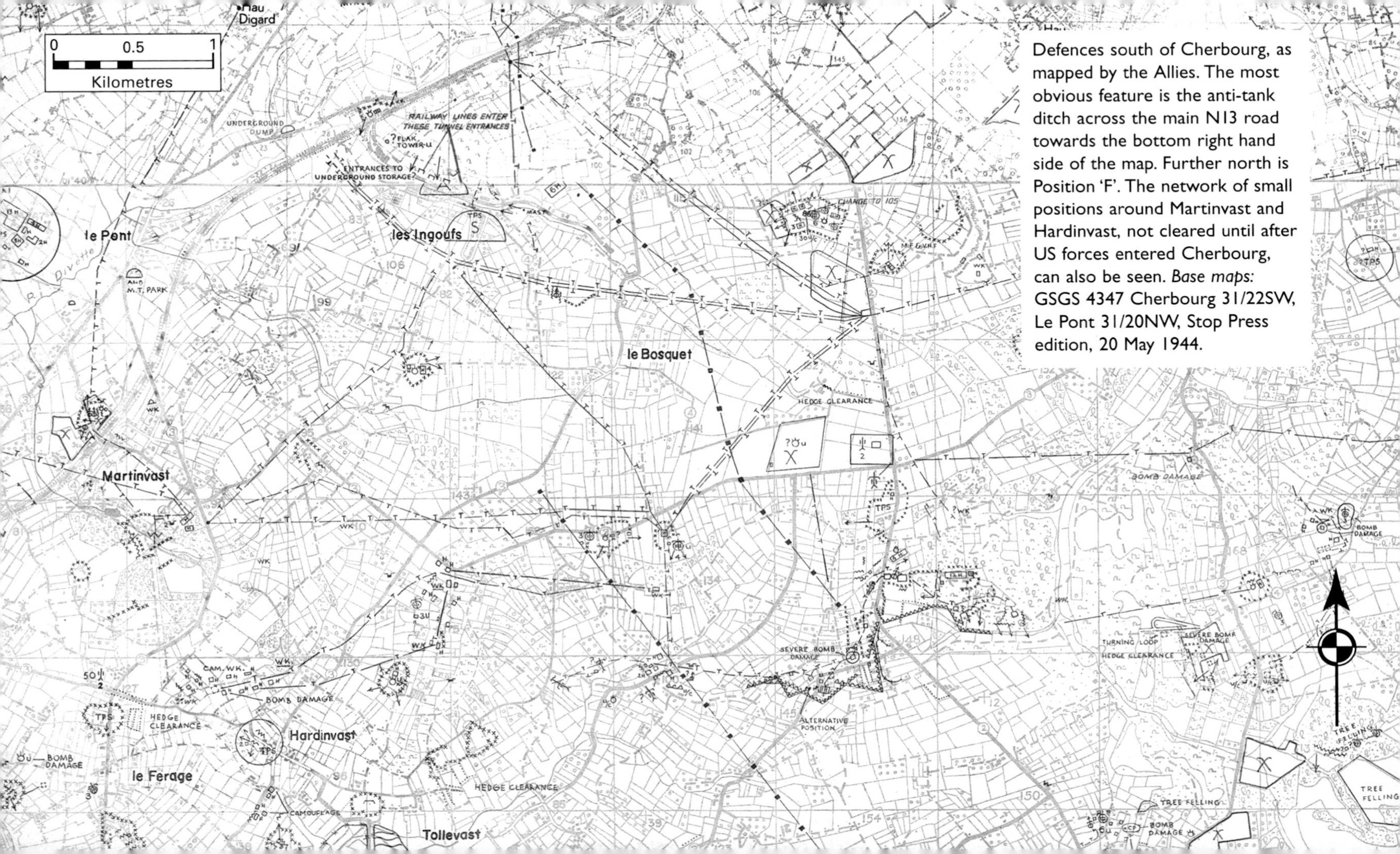

Defences south of Cherbourg, as mapped by the Allies. The most obvious feature is the anti-tank ditch across the main N13 road towards the bottom right hand side of the map. Further north is Position 'F'. The network of small positions around Martinvast and Hardinvast, not cleared until after US forces entered Cherbourg, can also be seen. *Base maps:* GSGS 4347 Cherbourg 31/22SW, Le Pont 31/20NW, Stop Press edition, 20 May 1944.

south, astride the main road and via a number of German fortifications. Of these, the most impressive were the strongpoint at les Chèvres, Position F (2 km north of les Chèvres) and the Fort du Roule, which was known to the Americans as Position D. These were defended by a mixture of personnel, among them anti-aircraft gunners, artillerymen and the remnants of 739th Grenadier Regiment (709th Infantry Division). The commander of the German forces facing the Americans in this sector was *Oberst* Köhn, CO of 739th Grenadiers.

The drive north began at 1400 hours on 22 June, following a massive concentration of air power against the German positions all around Cherbourg. Rocket-firing Typhoon fighter-bombers from the RAF's Second Tactical Air Force delivered the first wave of attacks at 1240 hours, followed by RAF Mustangs. At 1300 hours the US Ninth Air Force took over, with 562 aircraft (mainly P-47 Thunderbolts and P-38 Lightnings) participating in a series of low-level bombing and strafing runs. These continued into the early afternoon, with medium bombers joining the assault at 1400 hours. Sadly, losses to the dense flak were very heavy (367th Fighter Group alone lost eight P-38s, with all of the pilots killed). Furthermore, although damage was undoubtedly done to the German defences, many of the bombs landed behind US lines; Allied aircraft also machine-gunned American troops at several locations.

The 79th Division's attack employed all three of its infantry regiments, with 315th Infantry (Colonel Porter Wiggins) furthest west, near Tollevast, and 314th Infantry (Colonel Warren Robinson) on its right flank. Colonel Sterling Wood's 313th Infantry Regiment attacked astride the Valognes–Cherbourg highway, with the objective of clearing the position at les Chèvres and advancing beyond the crossroads at Point 177, 750 metres further north.

Soon after launching its attack, 1/313th Infantry ran into trouble from pillboxes in the les Chèvres position. However, 3/313th quickly pushed up, assaulting the German strongpoint from the flank while 1st Battalion maintained its frontal attack. With the main German position in US hands, the 313th then re-organised before resuming its advance north. Although 2/313th became badly disorganised while clearing German resistance in a densely forested area east of the highway, the rest of the regiment managed to occupy the crossroads at Point 177, and by 0205 hours on 23 June had established a front 400 metres beyond it. Here, it was joined by 3/314th Infantry, which had advanced around the western edge of the les Chèvres strongpoint during the late evening of the 22nd.

Stand C3: Crossroads 177 and Position F (la Mare à Canards)

DIRECTIONS: Rejoin the N13 heading north. After only a few hundred metres, and only if it appears safe to do so, pull up on the hard standing to your right, south of the location where the D122 road passes under the N13.

This photo, taken from slightly north of Crossroads 177, shows the area occupied by 313th Infantry Regiment early on the morning of 23 June. A modern roundabout marks the spot. *(Author)*

ORIENTATION: Immediately ahead of you is Crossroads or Point 177, where the modern D122 passes under the N13 (as a result of a modern survey, the tour map identifies this as Point 173). About 1.5 km further north, to the west of the N2013, is the location of Position F, another significant German strongpoint. Unfortunately, this position is now buried under modern buildings, and despite the presence of a large bunker beside the main road slightly south of position F, is not worth visiting. Owing to the lack of safe parking in this area, the action at Position F on 23–24 June is described below.

THE ACTION: On 23 June, 79th Infantry Division continued its attack towards Cherbourg. A strong effort was made by 314th Infantry, which attacked Position F at 1100 hours from the south-west. However, 3/314th Infantry was driven off by German fire, and although 1/314th penetrated beyond the strongpoint's western flank, fear that it would be caught in a planned air bombardment meant that it was ordered to withdraw early the next morning. Company A, however, remained in position near the village of la Loge. Meanwhile, 313th Infantry pushed up the main road from the south, but ran first into heavy German artillery fire, and was then dive-bombed by Allied aircraft. Although the reason for this incident is unclear, it appears that a failure to inform the 313th in a timely fashion that its attack should be delayed by several hours meant that, when the Allied aircraft arrived, its troops were already in the target area. The resulting casualties were heavy, and all attempts to capture Position F were abandoned for the day.

At 0825 hours on 24 June, following another air bombardment by 12 P-47 Thunderbolts, the Americans tried again. This time the attack was successful, with 2/314th Infantry overrunning a small position east of the main road at 0943 hours, and 3/314th Infantry capturing the main strongpoint by 1000. Following this success the 314th drove 750 metres further north, occupying the ridge 1.5 km south-east of the Fort du Roule. However, attempts by the 3rd Battalion to establish itself on the Montagne du Roule all failed in the face of constant machine-gun and artillery fire from the Octeville area further to the west. Consequently, the regiment was ordered to hold its positions overnight, and to be prepared to attack again the following morning.

The German Seventh Army War Diary describes the struggle on 24 June.

'In Fortress Cherbourg bitter fighting continued. After the enemy had placed artillery fire on the city of Cherbourg and carried out heavy bombing attacks on the Fort du Roule, his tank advances west of la Glacerie and south of Digosville were stemmed and dispersed. Then during the afternoon the enemy effected penetrations from the south and south-east into the defence line... The numerous losses of unit leaders, heaviest artillery fire and ceaseless air attacks have lately been causing a general reduction in our capacity to resist... Owing to the rupture of most communication and signal lines a coordinated command is no longer feasible. Based on this development, it cannot be doubted any longer that the enemy will force a breakthrough into the heart of the city on 25 June with his massed tanks and artillery... Commander-in-Chief West orders that the port and heart of the Fortress are to be defended to the last with all available forces. Strong points and pockets of resistance that are cut off will fight independently to the last round. The point at issue is to engage and destroy large enemy forces... and to prevent the enemy's attempt to render the port usable. This mission of the Fortress Commander is of historical importance.'

Source: Seventh Army War Diary; RG 407, Box 24154, Folder 488, US National Archives.

US troops dug in at Crossroads 177, probably in the two days following its capture on 22 June 1944.

The attack north beyond Crossroads 177 brought 314th Infantry Regiment to within several hundred metres of the main German communications centre for the entire Cherbourg *Landfront*. The communications facilities were located in a bunker and by-passed by the Americans in their efforts to seize ground and harass the retreating Germans. The undisturbed bunker continued to operate for several days, unbeknown to the Americans, and passed on information about US movements and activities in its vicinity. Unfortunately, despite considerable efforts, the author was unable to locate its precise whereabouts.

Stand C4: Upper levels, Fort du Roule

DIRECTIONS: Continue north towards Cherbourg, taking care to join the N2013 at the roundabout 400 metres beyond the D122/N13 crossing point (the N13 veers north-east to Tourlaville here). After a series of sharp bends that take you down into the valley immediately south of the Montagne du Roule, look for an even sharper right turn onto the D410 towards la Glacerie. Follow this road uphill for just over 1 km, stopping at the hard standing next to the *Maison Accueil Specialisée* on the right. Walk back downhill along the road for 25 metres until you see a track leading up onto the *montagne* to the right (north). Follow this track to the gate in the fence at the top and go through. Ahead of you is a very large quarry. Although the hazard is obvious enough (in places there are fences and warning signs), please do not stray from clearly defined trails in this area, and do obey any official notices posted at the time of your visit.

The narrow track leading towards the path up the southern slope of the Montagne du Roule. *(Author)*

Turn left and follow the track towards the fort's upper levels, which are located about 1 km to the north-west. Note that, at the time of the US assault, the whole area was cleared of vegetation in order to provide the defenders with uninterrupted fields of fire. Today the situation is very different, with much of the area covered with dense brush, small trees and long grass. For this reason tourers are advised to stick to the walking paths even though in places these only approximate to the routes taken by the attacking infantry. Furthermore, although German positions are very much in evidence, many are buried beneath brambles and other plants. Given that it took the author well over an hour to navigate his way to the fort's upper levels, it is probably best to save any investigations for your trip back downhill.

At the head of the track up the Montagne du Roule is a trail to the left, which should be followed. Directly ahead is a pleasant view over what is now a quarry to the eastern suburbs of Cherbourg and beyond. *(Author)*

THE SITE: The French military still uses part of the Fort du Roule, and the position's upper levels are therefore surrounded by a wire fence. Nevertheless, a visit to the Montagne du Roule cannot fail to reward the visitor keen to appreciate some of the problems faced by the Americans as they attacked over this ground on 25 June 1944. Furthermore, from the western side of the ridge it is possible to get an excellent view across the valley of the River Divette to the heights of Octeville, from which the Germans poured heavy fire onto the US troops as they assaulted the fort.

The Fort du Roule was originally built by the French as part of Cherbourg's defences, and in June 1944 was occupied by 5th Battery, 260th Naval Artillery Detachment (*Marine-Artillerie-Abteilung 260*). The battery's four 105-mm guns were emplaced in firing positions built into the cliff-face overlooking Cherbourg. These were connected to the upper levels of the fort by underground galleries that were almost impervious to the effects of Allied fire. On the roof of the fort itself there were three 20-mm anti-aircraft guns in open concrete emplacements, while the approaches along the ridge to the south-east were blocked by an anti-tank ditch and several machine-gun nests. Other defensive works, including flak positions, trenches and barbed wire fences, stretched along the *montagne* and down its southern slopes.

The Cherbourg suburb of Octeville is visible across the valley to the west from the upper levels of the Fort du Roule. At the left of the picture is an old bunker, positioned to defend against attempts to take the fort from the south. The large water tower is on a hill in Octeville. *(Author)*

THE ACTION: At 0800 hours on 25 June the Americans made their first attempts to take the Fort du Roule. A squadron of P-47s swooped down, machine-gunning and bombing the fort, but little physical damage appears to have been done to the defences. The soldiers of 2/314th and 3/314th Infantry then attacked across open ground over the re-entrant that lay 700 metres south of the fortress. The Americans faced a blizzard of small arms fire from defenders dug in along a track on the forward slope (now the D410 road). Concentrated machine-gun fire from the two US battalions managed to silence these

This excellent aerial shot, looking north, shows Fort du Roule after its capitulation. In the background lie the main basins of the port of Cherbourg. The heavy pounding that the fort received from air, sea and land bombardment is very apparent. The square concrete building in the centre of the picture is today the location of Cherbourg's *Musée de la Liberation*. (USNA)

positions, and elements of 2nd Battalion then took the lead, mopping up a motor transport pool and heading up onto the ridge. Here, around 150 prisoners were rounded up by E Company, while F Company also began edging towards the final objective at the western end of the Montagne du Roule.

Partly covered by fire from 3/314th Infantry south of the fort, the attackers used Bangalore torpedoes and demolition charges to clear blockhouses and other German positions. During this phase, acts of conspicuous gallantry earned Corporal John D. Kelly (E/314th Infantry) the highest US award for bravery in action, the Medal of Honor.

Corporal Kelly's Medal of Honor citation describes what happened.

'Kelly volunteered to try and knock out [a] strong point. Arming himself with a pole charge about ten feet long, with 15 pounds of TNT affixed, he climbed the slope

under a withering blast of machine gun fire and placed the charge at the strong point's base. The subsequent blast was ineffective and again, alone and unhesitatingly, he braved the slope to repeat the operation. This second blast blew off the ends of the enemy guns. Corporal Kelly then climbed the slope a third time to place a pole charge at the strong point's rear entrance. When this had been blown open he hurled hand grenades inside the position forcing the survivors of the enemy gun crews to come out and surrender.'

Kelly was killed in November 1944, and he was therefore awarded his medal posthumously.

The drop on the western side of the Montagne du Roule overlooking Cherbourg's rail station from the approach road to the fort. US troops clambered around these slopes in order to gain access to the lower levels. *(Author)*

Owing to heavy fire from positions higher up in the fort and from German defences near Octeville, at 1045 hours 3/314th Infantry was ordered to move forward to reinforce the attack and to clear resistance on 2nd Battalion's left flank. During this action another Medal of Honor was won, this time by 1st Lieutenant Carlos C. Ogden. For details of Ogden's part in the action see pages 78–9.

Following a day of difficult and bloody fighting, at 2148 hours white flags finally appeared above the remaining strongpoints on the surface of the Fort du Roule, and the garrison of the upper levels surrendered. However, not until the following day were the lower levels finally induced to capitulate (*see pages 79 and 81*). Until then, the guns emplaced there were able to cause some difficulty for 313th Infantry Regiment and other American units entering the eastern part of the city.

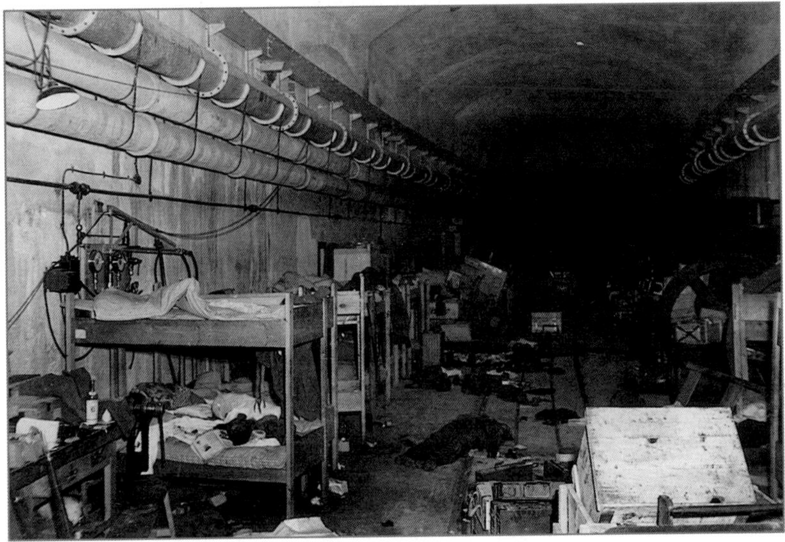

Part of the complex of tunnels beneath the Fort du Roule, photographed on 28 June. The bodies of some of the machinists who used these sleeping quarters lie on the floor. *(USNA)*

313th Infantry Regiment's history describes the fighting on 26 June and the attempts to silence the guns of the Fort du Roule.

'On the morning of 26 June the Regiment attacked Fortress Cherbourg in its zone of action and reached its objective at the beach about 0800. It encountered considerable sporadic resistance in moving through the streets and captured 1128 prisoners. There was occasional sniping during the day, much firing from the battery of guns below [in the lower levels of] the Fort du Roule and the 1st Battalion encountered serious opposition from the east portion of the Dock de Normandie. Four heavy concrete pillboxes delayed the advance for some hours. These were finally neutralised by small arms and mortar fire from 1st Battalion and battered into surrendering by anti-tank guns. Two platoons of Company A, 746th Tank Battalion, fired 75-mm guns against these pillboxes with

Captain W.H. Hooper (I Company, 314th Infantry Regiment) and his men escorting a long line of bedraggled Germans out of Cherbourg to the south. The famous Cherbourg sign is in the background. Captain Hooper was killed in the later fighting for la Haye-du-Puits. *(USNA)*

little visible result. From 1830 hours 26 June until 1845 [a] concentration of 57-mm anti-tank guns was directed against the battery of enemy guns located in the cliff below the Fort du Roule; these guns were silenced.'

Source: 313th Infantry Regiment history, 79th Division combat interviews; RG 407, Box 24033, Folder 153, US National Archives.

TO CONCLUDE THE TOUR: Retrace your steps to your vehicle and drive back to the N2013. Turn right towards the city centre and port area; the road here is known as the Avenue de Paris. Follow this road for about 500 metres, passing the famous 'Cherbourg' sign, fixed to the wall on the right hand (eastern) side of the street. Nearby, at the junction with the Avenue Étienne Lecarpentier, turn right. Within 100 metres turn right again and

The 'Cherbourg' sign today. *(Author)*

Cherbourg Liberation Museum

Musée de la Liberation, Fort du Roule, F-50100 Cherbourg-Octeville; tel: +33 (0)2 33 20 14 12. Open 1000–1800 daily (tourist season); 0930–1200 & 1400–1730 daily, except Mondays (winter). Admission charge.

head uphill, following the signs to the Fort du Roule. At the top of the zig-zag road, within the buildings of the fort, you will find the *Cherbourg Liberation Museum*, which holds numerous exhibits relevant to the subject matter covered in this book.

TOUR D

CLEARING THE CAP DE LA HAGUE

OBJECTIVE: This tour covers aspects of the American advance west from Cherbourg, during which 9th Infantry Division cleared the Cap de la Hague peninsula. It also examines some of the German fortifications on the western edge of Cherbourg.

DURATION/SUITABILITY: The tour covers about 21 km (from the parking location at Stand D1 to the D901 roundabout after Stand D5), with an optional extension at the end to the site of the German railway battery at Auderville-Laye. Altogether, the tour should last about a day. Although there are some hills, much of the ground covered is relatively gentle and the tour (but probably not the extension) is therefore suitable for cyclists. Tourers with mobility difficulties should note the walk to reach Stand D1 and the possibility of problematic access to Stand D2.

Stand D1: Digue de Querqueville

DIRECTIONS: From central Cherbourg drive west along the D45 coast road towards Equeurdreville, passing the bastions of the old naval arsenal on your right. As you do so look out for the remains of a German flak position at the northern end of the

a Digue centrale
b Naval arsenal
1 Flak position
2 Fort des Couplets (Equeurdreville fortress); see pp. 79-80
3 Battery York
4 Defensive positions
Base map: IGN 1210OT
Urville-Nacqueville
QUERQUEVILLE
EQUEURDREVILLE
Fort de Querqueville
Pointe de Querqueville
Digue de Querqueville
Fort de Chavagnac
Fort de l'Ouest
Phare
Passe de l'Ouest
Baie de Querqueville
Baie de Ste-Anne
Anse de Querqueville
Rocher de Nacqueville
Cité Dixmude
Hameau de la Mer
Ste-Anne
Hameau Bourgeois
Fort des Couplets
D1
D2
D45
D118
0
0.5
1

arsenal walls (this can more easily be seen from the cycle path alongside the road), as well as further defensive positions on the slopes overlooking the coast. About 500 metres beyond the roundabout at Cité Dixmude turn right towards the Fort de Querqueville. Park near or adjacent to the laid-up ex-French Navy corvette (visible from the approach road), and then walk towards the harbour breakwater, the Digue de Querqueville.

THE SITE: At the beginning of the breakwater, pause to look north-west to the nineteenth century Fort de Querqueville, which was incorporated into the German defences of Cherbourg. Then proceed for a kilometre along the breakwater until you can go no further, passing assembled ranks of French fishermen *en route*. At the end of the *digue*, look south for a reasonably close view of the Fort de Chavagnac. Although the strength of such a position when it was first built (during the Napoleonic Wars) is evident, it is equally obvious that by 1944, confronting an enemy in full control of the skies, such positions were much more vulnerable to attack. Looking south-east, you also have unobstructed views of the Fort du Roule, which dominates Cherbourg from the south. The main reason for coming this far along the breakwater, however, is to get as close as possible to the Fort de l'Ouest, which can be seen 1.1 km east of your position, at the western end of the Digue Centrale.

The Fort de Chavagnac on 2 July 1944, just days after the surrender of German forces in Cherbourg. Here we can see two French cannon in the fort, both dating from 1884 and unlikely to have taken much part in the fighting 60 years later.

An even better view of the fort can be gained from the cross-Channel ferries that pass through the western harbour entrance several times each day. However, this position is the closest that one can achieve from the land.

The Fort de Chavagnac, looking south from the extreme end of the Digue de Querqueville, with Cherbourg's western suburbs beyond. *(Author)*

THE ACTION: It was to the Fort de l'Ouest that the German harbour commander at Cherbourg, *Fregattenkapitän* Hermann Witt, a *Kriegsmarine* officer, escaped at 0330 hours on 27 June 1944, accompanied by eight officers and 30 men. Witt and his men made their perilous journey from the naval arsenal aboard a small yacht and two rowing boats (motor boats risked setting off the sonic detonators of some of the harbour mines), with the aim of being in a position to detonate the demolition charges at the western entrance to the harbour, the control mechanism for which was housed in the Fort de l'Ouest. Witt's mission might have been a success, and a major shock to the Allies, had not someone at German Seventh Army passed on news of Witt's position. German propaganda made much of the story, making Witt a hero, but also inadvertently telling the Americans, who were monitoring German broadcasts, Witt's location and intentions. US artillery fire and air power destroyed the electrical connection from the Fort de l'Ouest to the detonators, obliging Witt to surrender, his mission unaccomplished, on the afternoon of 29 June.

The final fort seen during the tour of the Digue de Querqueville is the most famous of all, the scene of *Fregattenkapitän* Witt's epic, but futile, last-ditch effort to demolish even more of Cherbourg's port capacity. The Fort de l'Ouest is the nearest, and clearest of the several in view here. *(Author)*

The 12th Infantry Regiment had been allocated the unenviable task of assaulting the forts along the Digue Centrale amphibiously, should the US bombardment fail. Its regimental history offers a fascinating account of the events that led to Witt's surrender.

'In spite of the two day bombardment, there were only three German casualties. One of them happened to be a Lt Col. The other [*sic*] was the supreme commander of the fortress defences [probably Witt, who received a chest wound]. It was undoubtedly due to the plight of these two Prussians that the forts surrendered as quickly as they did. Close examination showed the physical proportions of the fort were so firmly constructed that they might well have withstood a 50 day siege. The forts were five stories deep, three below the waterline and two above. The stone and concrete walls were six feet thick. Ample food and water and small arms ammunition was stored deep in the lower levels.

It was only due to a series of lucky accidents that the [German] commanders were wounded. Many rounds of 155-mm (Long Tom) shells skilfully aimed at the apertures managed to blast their way into Fort West's walls. Several

German grenades exploded due to sympathetic detonation. Ironically the German shrapnel wounded the two commanders who quite by chance happened to be in the same room at just the right time. Another well aimed shell blasted its way deep into the wall and cut the main control wires of the fort and damaged beyond repair the generator and control panel which operated the mine switchboard. Even the Prussian leaders could see no further reason for attempting to hold the now useless forts. It was due to the above related accident, a goodly amount of luck and judicious planning that the battle of the forts was a bloodless one.'

Source: 12th Infantry Regiment history, 4th Infantry Division combat interviews; RG 407, Box 24014, Folder 29, US National Archives.

Stand D2: German coastal battery 'York' (the Amfréville or Querqueville Battery)

DIRECTIONS: Return to the D45 coast road and drive west for roughly 2 km. At la Rivière turn left and immediately left again, heading uphill towards Amfréville. After 600 metres, at a T-junction, turn left again. You can park either on the left or right of the road, in front of the houses stretching along the D118 towards Querqueville. Walk eastwards for a short distance (no more than 200 metres) until you reach a gateway on the northern side of the road, through which access is possible into the extensive remains of the 'York' Battery. Since it is unclear whether or not you have a legal right of access, you should be very careful not to disrupt any farming activity, and should be prepared to leave the site immediately if asked. Furthermore, although the casemates and other structures appear to be in reasonably good condition, you should observe the safety guidelines on visiting fortifications given on pages 112–4.

THE SITE: This is the location of one of at least half a dozen major artillery positions that existed between the western edge of Cherbourg and the tip of the Cap de la Hague peninsula in June 1944. The battery that was located here consisted of four 170-mm SKL/40 guns mounted in casemates, and was operated by the German Navy (its full designation was 8th Battery, 260th

Naval Artillery Detachment). The guns here, although not of the very largest size, were nevertheless powerful pieces with a 27-km (17-mile) range. A number of 75-mm anti-tank guns, mortars and machine guns protected the battery against attack from the landward side, while the entire position was surrounded by wire entanglements and fences. The location of the main battery observation post is unknown, although it may have been on a piece of high ground 200 metres west of the gun casemates, on the other side of the road by which you originally approached the position.

A view, looking east, of the main tower of the German positions near Amfréville, the 'York' battery. This position is very well preserved, with the obvious exception of the guns themselves, which have long since disappeared. (*Author*)

THE ACTION: The battery here, together with several others west of Cherbourg, was heavily involved in the artillery duel that took place on 25 June with Allied naval forces under the command of Rear Admiral Morton L. Deyo (*see also pages 143–5*). It was initially fired on by the Royal Navy 6-inch cruisers HMS *Glasgow* and HMS *Enterprise*, using air spotting, and later by the US 8-inch cruisers *Tuscaloosa* and *Quincy* and the 14-inch guns of the battleship USS *Nevada*. Several US destroyers also contributed to the bombardment. Nevertheless, despite temporary interruptions to their fire, the German naval gunners stayed at their posts and at least one gun was still shooting when the Allied ships withdrew at 1500 hours. Although it is uncertain whether Battery York registered any hits, it may have been responsible for damage to HMS *Glasgow*, which was struck twice just before 1300 hours.

With the Americans in Cherbourg, it seems that the Germans chose to abandon the gun position at Querqueville. Although several hundred prisoners were taken by 2nd Battalion, 47th Infantry Regiment, (9th Division) when it advanced to the coast on 27 June, most of these were rounded up around Hainneville, some 2 km to the south-east. According to US records, when Querqueville itself was occupied by 1/47th Infantry the following day, very few Germans were found in the area. It is possible that the naval gunners moved west to join the final defence of the Cap de la Hague, which is covered at the next three stands.

Stand D3: Landemer

DIRECTIONS: Retrace your route to the D45. At la Rivière turn left and drive along the D45 for about 4.5 km, passing through Urville-Nacqueville before taking the right hand turn to Landemer, which is well signposted. Continue along the road to the cliff-top viewing point 750 metres away and park there.

ORIENTATION: From this position, which is marked on Allied 1944 intelligence maps as an observation post or resistance nest, there are excellent views along the coast to the west. By looking very slightly inland towards the higher ground 700 metres away (marked on modern maps as Castel Vendon), you can also see the area occupied by another important (if incomplete) German coastal artillery battery. This was known as 'Marine Battery Landemer', although its official title was 6th Battery, 260th Naval Artillery Detachment. According to the Germans it was equipped with four 150-mm guns; one US account, however, states that three 8-inch (203-mm) guns were captured here when the position was taken on the evening of 29 June. The battery was one of several that participated in the action against Admiral Deyo's ships on 25 June, and was itself shelled during that fight.

THE ACTION: Following the fall of Cherbourg, on 27–28 June the 9th Infantry Division regrouped for operations to clear the Cap de la Hague peninsula. The attack was to be conducted by

47th Infantry Regiment, which would advance westwards to the north of the main east–west road (now the D901), and 60th Infantry Regiment, which was to launch its assault along the main road itself. The offensive was to be supported by 4th Cavalry Reconnaissance Squadron, mopping up along the southern coast of the peninsula, and 39th Infantry Regiment, which initially was in reserve. Tanks, artillery and air power were to assist the American drive west.

Opposing the US forces were the remnants of several German units. These included *Unterkampfgruppe Hadenfelt*, comprising *Major* Hadenfelt's 2nd Battalion, 919th Grenadiers (by now, reduced to about 250 men) and 3rd Battalion, 919th Grenadiers (with fewer than 100 soldiers), plus five guns from 709th Division's anti-tank battalion. *Kampfgruppe Müller*, with the survivors of 922nd Grenadiers and 3rd Battalion, 920th Grenadiers, was also in the front line. In addition, five obsolescent French tanks were available, along with a few men from the Seventh Army Assault Battalion and some paratroopers, and a much larger number of flak and coastal artillery personnel. Altogether, German forces in the peninsula amounted to around 6,000 troops. Probably no more than a thousand of these men, however, were properly trained for ground combat.

The view towards the Cap de la Hague from Landemer. US infantry advanced across these undulating and sparsely wooded hills towards what was considered to be the impressively fortified *Westeck* around the villages of Gréville-Hague and Hameau Gruchy. *(Author)*

1 L/47th Infantry, 30 June
2 K/47th Infantry, 30 June
3 E/47th Infantry, 30 June
4 F/47th Infantry, 30 June
5 I/47th Infantry, 30 June
6 1/47th Infantry, 30 June
7 Battery Landemer
8 Westeck (Battle Group *Hadenfelt*)
9 Battle Group *Müller* positions
Base maps: IGN 1210OT
For further details of the extensive German defences within this area, see the 1944 Allied intelligence map on p.179
To JOBOURG, LAYE and AUDERVILLE
Gréville-Hague
Urville-Na
Hameau Gruchy
Hameau Cousin
Landemer
Castel Vendon
la Quiesce
Hameau Nicolle
Haut Hameau
Eudal de Bas
Eudal de Haut
Branville-Hague
Hameau Bosvy
Hameau Fleury
Hameau Samson
Hameau aux Ducs
Hameau Néel
Lieu Bailly
St-Nazaire
Lieu Piquot
D45
D237
D3
D4
D5
D901

On 29 June the Americans moved forward, clearing negligible opposition as they went. Closest to the coast, 3/47th Infantry reached the ridge that runs south-west from your viewing point. Following a short artillery bombardment at 2030 hours, the battalion then attacked Battery Landemer, which fell without significant opposition.

Two officers of 3/47th Infantry describe the action at Landemer.

'K and L Companies deployed for the attack, K as the assault company, initially, under Captain James D. Allgood. The forward defences were not defended, however, and there was no fight there. We took 40 PWs [prisoners of war], though. K and L then moved up... preparatory to further attack on the main position. At 1930 the Germans could be seen all over the real fortification... We received a great deal of artillery fire in our positions and the Colonel kept his battalion back until we would bring effective supporting fire on the positions.

We registered on the target with our cannon, and one battalion each of medium and light artillery at 2000. But there was trouble with communications, so we fired for effect with cannon and mortars only at first. At 2030 we got artillery fire and we took off, K initially assaulting on the left, L on the right, I to the left rear. We took the fortification, captured three guns and 250 PWs.'

Source: 9th Division combat interview (20 July 1944); RG 407, Box 24026, Folder 53, US National Archives.

Stand D4: Hameau Gruchy (the Westeck)

DIRECTIONS: Retrace your route to the D45 and turn right, continuing west for about 2 km past the site of Battery Landemer on your right; there is a track to the position if you wish to visit it. Just past the battery there is a slightly complicated road junction at the northern end of the village of la Quiesce. Here, continue bearing right along the D45 for about 50 metres and then turn right on the minor road to Hameau Gruchy. Drive slowly, crossing a small stream after about 250 metres. This stream represented the line of departure for 3/47th Infantry's attack on the village of Gruchy on 30 June. If it is safe to do so, pause here, trying to envisage the troops of L Company and a platoon of K Company deployed to your right, on the western bank of the stream between you and the coast, with the rest of K Company to your left and I Company behind you. Then continue uphill to Hameau Gruchy, driving along the route followed by the American infantry as they attacked the Germans at the top of the hill.

THE SITE: Hameau Gruchy was part of the German position known as the *Westeck*, which was generally regarded as the strongest point in the whole Cap de la Hague peninsula. It was defended by *Unterkampfgruppe Hadenfelt*, and comprised anti-tank guns, underground bunkers (some with tank turrets on top) and trench systems. There was also a radar station on the north-west edge of the position, while almost the whole site was surrounded by an anti-tank ditch. Theoretically, the *Westeck* was supported by the defences of Battery Landemer to the east although, as described above, this position had already been captured when the Americans attacked the *Westeck* on 30 June.

THE ACTION: To take the *Westeck*, all three battalions of the 47th Infantry were employed. 3/47th attacked Gruchy, while 2/47th launched an assault on Gréville-Hague, 1 km to the south-west. 1/47th also participated in the attack, although at first with limited effect.

At Gruchy, 3/47th's K and L Companies moved forward at about 0800 hours, following a heavy artillery and mortar preparation; a planned bombing mission, however, was cancelled owing to bad weather. Resistance was determined, and the leading troops came under intense mortar fire (some of which appears to have come from an unusual 50-mm mortar mounted on a turntable, which was capable of firing six rounds at a time). Nevertheless, by 1200 hours the Americans had reached the eastern edge of the village, where they again came under fire from German positions along the ridge to the west and the south.

Following a second artillery and mortar bombardment, some of it provided by 2/47th Infantry near Gréville-Hague, K and L Companies pushed forward through the village, clearing the main German position by 1500 hours. Meanwhile, I Company shifted south-west along the stream bed at the line of the departure, before swinging west along the road into Gréville, and

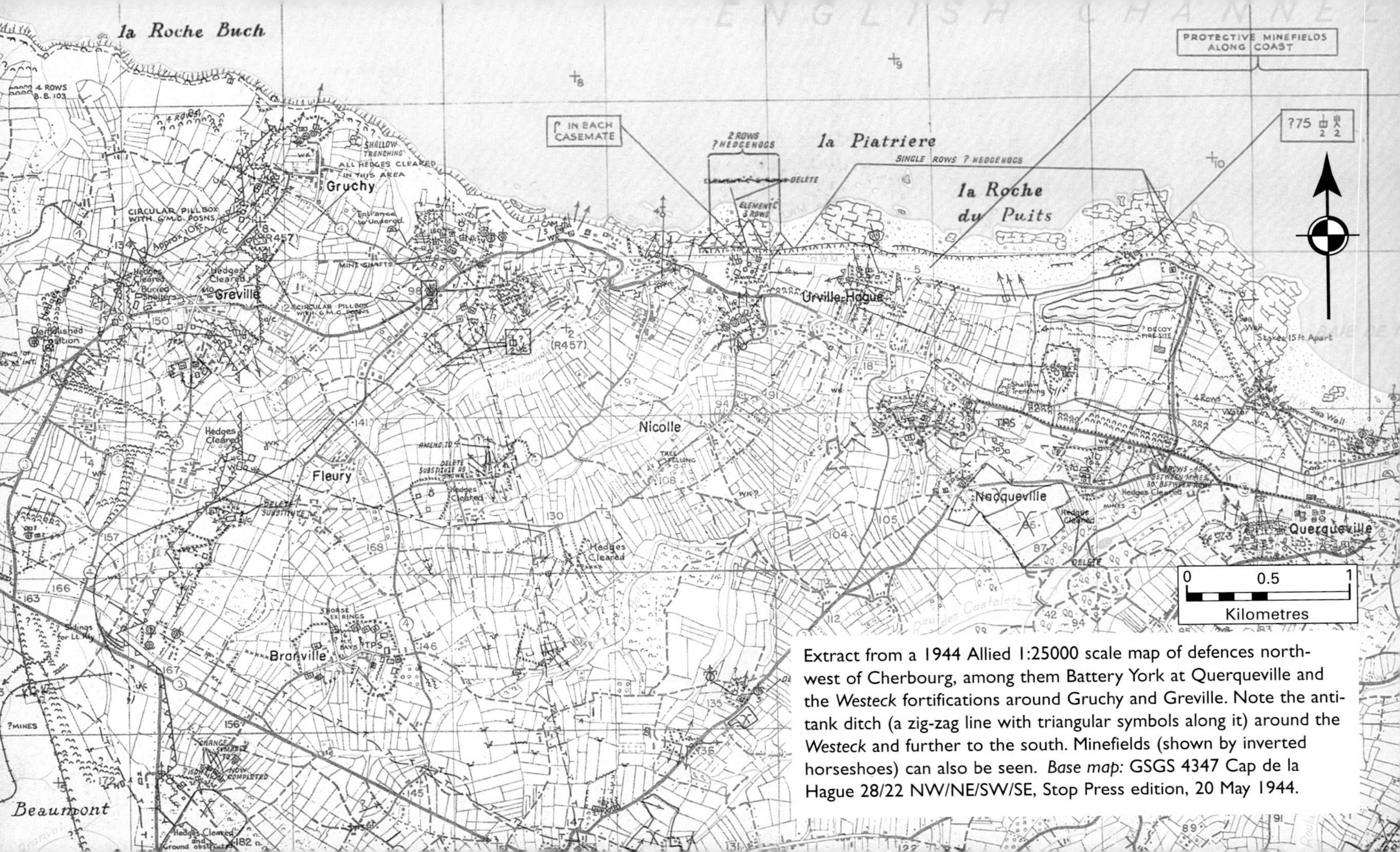

Extract from a 1944 Allied 1:25000 scale map of defences north-west of Cherbourg, among them Battery York at Querqueville and the *Westeck* fortifications around Gruchy and Greville. Note the anti-tank ditch (a zig-zag line with triangular symbols along it) around the *Westeck* and further to the south. Minefields (shown by inverted horseshoes) can also be seen. *Base map:* GSGS 4347 Cap de la Hague 28/22 NW/NE/SW/SE, Stop Press edition, 20 May 1944.

from here to the farm buildings at Hameau aux Ducs. During this phase German resistance began to crumble, and numerous prisoners gave themselves up as the Americans advanced through Gruchy towards the coast beyond. By 1700 hours 3/47th Infantry claimed to have captured all its objectives, along with 500 prisoners. Its own casualties amounted to 65 men.

Stand D5: Gréville-Hague

DIRECTIONS: At the crossroads at the western edge of Gruchy turn left (south) on the D237 and continue for 1 km into the centre of Gréville-Hague. Driving along this road, you are effectively following the eastward-facing main defence line held by the Germans on 30 June, with the Americans attacking through the fields to your left. In Gréville, park where it is safe to do so. There is an interesting plaque in the small village square (at the confluence of all the significant routes into the village) dedicated to civilians killed in the course of the war. For those in need of refreshment, the small bar-tabac *l'Angelus* is very good value, which is fortunate since it is the only restaurant in the immediate area. Walk eastwards past the church along the D45, and then turn right onto a minor road that bends 90 degrees before heading steadily downhill. Go past the buildings on your left and right until you are in a position to see a reasonable distance down the road in front of you.

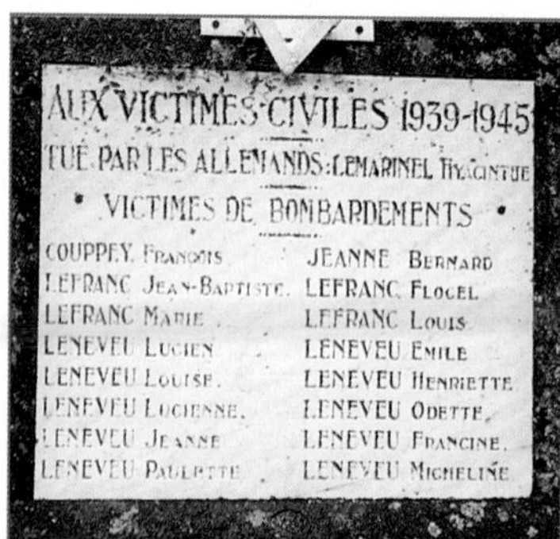

The plaque dedicated to civilian victims in the small village square in Gréville-Hague. *(Author)*

ORIENTATION: 500 metres away from the edge of Gréville-Hague is the same stream from which 3/47th Infantry launched its attack on Gruchy further to the north. In this case you are viewing the axis of attack from the German positions on the eastern perimeter of the *Westeck*, rather than from the US perspective. In 1944 an anti-tank ditch stretched across the road in front of you and there were several bunkers in the fields to your right. The stream in the valley to the east represented the line of departure for 2/47th Infantry, attacking uphill with E Company to the north and F Company to the south of the road (and G in reserve). Individual Sherman tanks supported two of the platoons of F Company, with a third in reserve; two tank destroyers fired from a position slightly further to the south.

The view from the Gréville-Hague–Hameau Gruchy road, which runs north to south, showing the terrain over which the Americans attacked (towards the camera). *(Author)*

THE ACTION: 2/47th's attack made rapid progress when it began at 0800 hours. By 0900 the battalion had entered Gréville, from which it advanced beyond the western end of the village. Here, however, it came under machine-gun and mortar fire from the Gruchy area (at this time, still in German hands) and bunkers at the western extremity of the *Westeck*.

Captain Otto Geyer, commanding F Company, 2/47th Infantry, describes the attack on Gréville.

'The outlying trenches had been abandoned during the artillery fire, making entrances for our men. Our men therefore used the trenches to work their way up to the town. Men pitched grenades for all they were worth, particularly Lieutenant MacDaniels who had just joined the Company. A hundred prisoners were taken in this way. In the trenches were found hundreds of Molotov cocktails which they [the Germans] had no opportunity to use. The right platoon got into town. A tank and grenades took a pillbox south of town. Then we got mortar fire from north and east and from high ground to our west. Captain Geyer managed to get in a German command post with a periscope, [and] used it to bring mortar and artillery (84th Field Artillery Battalion) fire on the position north and east, using a radio for communication. The 1st Battalion, to our south, tried to get around the town... [but] was pinned down. We laid smoke on the German positions for them. But the 1st Battalion (whose CO was in the command post with Captain Geyer) failed to attack (he was relieved). By 1100 we had Gréville, but the Germans were still holding to the west.'

Source: Interview (17 July 1944) with Captain Geyer, 9th Infantry Division combat interviews; RG 407, Box 24026, Folder 53, US National Archives.

Following the second US artillery bombardment in the early afternoon, and with 1/47th Infantry finally making progress around the enemy's southern flank, the garrison of the *Westeck* began to capitulate in large numbers. 3/47th's I Company, arriving from the north-east, reported the capture of 200 prisoners in Gréville, which it handed over to the 2/47th. Despite minor losses to mortar fire and mines, US tank destroyers and Sherman tanks also played an important role in demolishing pillboxes and other fortified positions at close range. Later in the evening 2/47th Infantry broke completely free of the *Westeck*, advancing several kilometres towards Digulleville before nightfall. According to German sources, however, some of the *Westeck*'s defenders remained in their bunkers until the following day, when the position was finally mopped up. Among them was the garrison commander, *Major* Hadenfelt, who surrendered at 1600 hours on 1 July.

With the capture of the *Westeck*, plus some hard-won gains by 60th Infantry Regiment along the D901 to the south, the German position in the Cap de la Hague peninsula finally collapsed. Moving up from reserve, 3/39th Infantry thrust forward north-west of Jobourg on the night of 30 June/1 July, and at 0500 hours on 1 July the battalion entered Auderville, near the peninsula's northern extremity, where it began rounding up the last of the defenders. Finally, the Battle for Cherbourg could be considered at an end.

A US regimental history comments on the end of the Battle for Cherbourg.

'The inhabitants began to creep back, bringing their belongings on every conveyance imaginable. The troops who had taken the city prepared for their departure. It was the time for them to leave, for the growing anti-climax was becoming more and more apparent. The brass and the brassards, the photographers and the Navy began to throng the rubble-littered but far less lethal streets. Everyone who wanted to say they were at Cherbourg began to arrive, so the troops moved out. They marched out with a spirit of high accomplishment, with pride in their deeds and those of their fallen comrades.'

Source: 313th Infantry Regiment history, 27 June – 15 July 1944, 79th Infantry Division combat interviews; RG 407, Box 24033, Folder 153, US National Archives.

The remains of one of the highly impressive 203-mm railway guns just inland of Laye after the concerted attentions of Allied aircraft. The photograph was taken on 5 July 1944 after the capture of the battery. *(USNA)*

TO CONCLUDE THE TOUR: Return to your vehicle and drive about 1 km south-west from Gréville-Hague along the D45 before turning left onto the D237. Follow this road for 1.75 km to the D901 dual carriageway, which you can use to return to Cherbourg by turning left (east) at the roundabout.

The site of the Laye battery today. The infrastructure of the gun positions still remains, albeit showing the effects of 60 years of Norman weather. There is no evidence today of the guns themselves but ammunition bunkers and other concrete structures are still standing. *(Author)*

Alternatively, if you wish to visit the site of another important German artillery battery of a rather unusual kind, head west towards Jobourg, 7 km away, on reaching the D901. As you do so, you are following the route used by 60th Infantry Regiment during its own advance. Its attack encountered strong resistance about 1 km east of the D237/D901 intersection (at the modern junction between the D901 and D37), but gathered momentum during the evening of 30 June. Continue past the vast nuclear reprocessing plant west of Beaumont-Hague and on through Jobourg. About 3 km north-west of Jobourg, immediately east of the coastal settlement of Laye and to the left of the D901, is a cluster of bunkers and other structures, which are clearly visible from the road. This is the site of 3rd Battery, 1262nd Army Coastal Artillery Regiment, which was equipped with two 203-mm guns, mounted on railway bogies. These guns, which had their coastal observation post at the *Westeck*, were capable of firing almost 40 km. The site today is accessible, though over several hedges, and is still recognisable as the location for large rail-mounted guns with the ammunition and crew bunkers still standing. There is parking nearby on the D901, on the hard standing beside the road.

PART FOUR

ON YOUR RETURN

FURTHER RESEARCH

If your interest has been whetted by this book or by following the recommended tours in Normandy and you wish to read more on the fighting for Cherbourg (and/or the battle for Normandy in general) then below is a list of additional reading, primary source archives and museums that may prove of interest. Obviously a very useful source of information for all aspects of the Normandy campaign are the other volumes in the 'Battle Zone Normandy' series.

Secondary source works that focus solely on the operations to seize Cherbourg are few. The best place to begin, in terms of accessible secondary source books, is William B. Breuer's *Hitler's Fortress Cherbourg: The Conquest of a Bastion* (New York, 1984). Also of interest is Paul Carell's *Invasion – They're Coming* (Boston, 1964) which features a dramatic (and dramatised) chapter on the fall of Cherbourg and its place in the overall battle for Normandy. For a very detailed, tactical, examination of VII Corps' activities up until the surrender of Cherbourg the best work is the US Department of the Army's official history *Utah Beach to Cherbourg* (Washington, 1947). This examines all elements of the fighting in the northern Cotentin and is a fine reference work but is not an easy read. Similarly, the substantial volumes of the United States Official History *World War Two* are very useful reference works, and examples of impeccable scholarship, but are not particularly light going. The two volumes that relate to this period are Gordon A. Harrison's *Cross Channel Attack* (Washington, 1951), which covers the D-Day landings and fighting for Cherbourg, and Martin Blumenson's *Breakout and Pursuit* (Washington, 1961), which incorporates the action of VIII Corps south towards la Haye-du-Puits. Of particular interest also is the autobiography of General Collins, *Lightning Joe*, (Baton Rouge, 1979). The fighting for Cherbourg was but one element in Collins' impressive career but the book is nonetheless illuminating on this subject. An interesting pictorial history of the battle for Cherbourg is *Première Victoire Americaine en Normandie* (no place of publication, 1990) by Georges Bernage.

Above: At Camp Patton a simple plaque and two flag posts commemorate the US efforts to liberate Normandy in the days after the allied invasion of 6 June 1944. In this photograph, taken in July, a small wreath of poppies has been placed in front of the memorial. *(Author)*

Page 185: In the aftermath of the German surrender in Cherbourg, Maj Gen J. Lawton Collins organised a 'victory parade' in the centre of the city. During this impressive ceremony on 27 June Collins handed over the city to the mayor and distributed liberation medals to his victorious soldiers. As can be seen from the photo the city square was packed with civilians, many of whom had escaped the fighting by fleeing, temporarily, into the surrounding countryside. *(USNA)*

This book has over 200 photographs, many of which are not usually seen, and is of considerable interest. At the time of writing there was no English language translation available but the photographs alone are worth looking at.

Works concerned with the Normandy battles in general are, predictably, numerous. Some of the better and more easily accessible include Carlo D'Este, *Decision in Normandy* (London, 1984) and Max Hastings, *Overlord*, (London, 1984). Russell Hart's *Clash of Arms: How the Allies Won in Normandy* (London, 2001) is a particularly good recent work on the subject. Other books either written by, or about, the major commanders involved in the Normandy campaign include Omar Bradley's *A Soldier's Story*, (New York, 1951); Steven Ambrose's biography of Eisenhower, *The Supreme Commander* (New York, 1970) and also Eisenhower's own *Crusade in Europe*, (New York, 1948); James Gavin, *On to Berlin* (New York, 1978); Walter Warlimont, *Inside Hitler's Headquarters* (New York, 1964). Also of tremendous use, and the source of much of the raw data on the structure and equipment of German units deployed in the fighting for Cherbourg, is *Normandy 1944: German Military Organization, Combat Power and Organizational Effectiveness* (Winnipeg, Canada, 2000) by Niklas Zetterling.

In terms of primary source archive material the US National Archives in Washington DC contains a vast repository of documents relating to US military activities in the Cotentin as well as copies of large numbers of translated German documents. Here it is possible to peruse individual unit war diaries from corps level down through division, regiment and battalion and to access thousands of personal accounts of the fighting. There are also many regimental/unit associations that can prove to be useful in establishing direct contact with survivors of the actual fighting. The internet is also a very worthwhile source of a tremendous amount of ephemera connected to the Second World War in general and specific engagements and units in particular.

In Britain the obvious starting points for research are the National Archives at Kew and the Imperial War Museum. In the United Kingdom another interesting site connected with the United States involvement in the D-Day landings is the American Cemetery at Madingley in Cambridgeshire. This war cemetery is magnificently maintained and an impressive construction on the lines of those in Normandy. It holds the remains of 3,812 US military personnel killed on active service in the European theatre and also has a memorial to 5,162 who have no known grave. Madingley is just outside Cambridge and the cemetery is well signposted from the M11 motorway.

Useful Addresses

Imperial War Museum, Lambeth Road London, SE1 6HZ; tel: 020 7416 5320; email: <mail@iwm.org.uk>; web: <www.iwm.org.uk>.

UK National Archives, Public Record Office, Kew, Richmond, Surrey TW9 4DU; tel: 020 8876 3444; email: <enquiry@nationalarchives.gov.uk>; web: <www.nationalarchives.gov.uk>.

US National Archives, The National Archives and Records Administration, 8601 Adelphi Road, College Park MD 20740–6001; tel: +01 866 272 6272; web: <www.archives.gov>.

Madingley American Military Cemetery, Coton, Cambridge CB3 7PH; tel: 01954 210350; web: <www.abmc.gov>.
Cambridge American Cemetery and Memorial is located 5 km west of Cambridge on the A1303. Open 0900–1700 daily, except 25 Dec & 1 Jan.

INDEX

Page numbers in *italics* denote an illustration.